Praise for

LAUREN GREUTMAN and

THE RECOVERING SPENDER

"Lauren brings an incredible amount of energy and fun to something other people consider a chore. She makes the frugal life an entertaining read with a refreshing amount of honesty and candor about her own financial challenges and solutions. Anyone looking to better support a family, pay off debt, or cut spending would do well to take some tips from Lauren." —Libby Kane, personal-finance editor, *Business Insider*

"Lauren Greutman is one of the most enterprising and self-motivated educators on the web! She speaks to the everyday consumer in a way that does not make them feel guilty or overwhelmed about running a household. We need more people like this in big finance!"

—Natali Morris, CNBC

"Lauren Greutman is my favorite source of information on how to save money and make better spending choices when it comes to daily expenses. Somehow she manages to make budgeting an enjoyable task—no easy feat. Her book is the perfect guide for anyone looking to take back control over their cash flow."

—Kimberly Palmer, author of *Smart Mom, Rich Mom*

"As a recovering overspender, I know that budgeting experts can be intimidating. Strict budgeting regimens can exacerbate the problem of why you are overspending in the first place and keep you from enjoying the money you do have. Lauren gets that! She wants us all to spend money wisely and get the most value and enjoyment out of every cent. Her method of budgeting is fun, approachable, and winnable."

—Clayton Morris, cohost, *FOX & Friends Weekend* on FOX News Channel

"There are countless personal finance 'experts' out there, but Lauren's honesty, smarts, and genuine commitment to helping other families blast through this overcrowded space. It's no secret to her business's quick rise: it's Lauren."

—Emma Johnson, *Forbes* columnist, creator of WealthySingleMommy.com

"*The Recovering Spender* is a compelling and definitive resource for those looking to reclaim their financial lives. Lauren Greutman has given us a meaningful and important book that demystifies complex financial ideas into understandable nuggets. These pages sparkle with Lauren's humor and passion."

—Kabir Sehgal, *New York Times* bestselling author of *Coined: The Rich Life of Money and How Its History Has Shaped Us*

"Lauren's story is one that needs to be shared. Her ability to overcome a spending addiction and dig her family out of debt is truly inspiring and should serve as a motivational guide to others who are struggling with their own money issues."

—Cameron Huddleston, award-winning personal-finance journalist at Kiplinger

"Lauren inspires families across the country to live life well without putting their finances at risk. Her writing is fun and engaging and the fact that she teaches through her own life experiences makes it all that much easier to relate to her advice."

—Mandi Woodruff, personal-finance correspondent and executive editor at MagnifyMoney

"Time to change your spending ways? Get ready! Lauren is your personal, go-to guide. She knows the steps it will take to break your bad habits and achieve real financial success." —Philip Taylor, founder and CEO, FinCon

"Lauren Greutman is an award-winning personal-finance writer and has been featured on dozens of top financial websites. She makes boring topics like 'budgeting' and 'frugal living' easy to understand and fun. I'm grateful for her passion and financial-literacy work."

—Michael Delgado, Experian

"Lauren Greutman is a guru who's been there and lived to tell about it. No sound bites, no clichés, just helpful, digestible advice"

—Joe Saul-Sehy, *Stacking Benjamins* podcast

"Lauren's message is as infectious as it is inspiring. Debt is overwhelming, but Lauren truly knows how to connect with her readers in a way that will inspire success through simple step-by-step actions. Getting out of debt is possible for anyone, and Lauren has been teaching audiences exactly how to do it by employing real-world smart-spending strategies. As a fellow consumer expert, I'm in awe of the enormous audiences Lauren has been able to reach with her message."

—Josh Elledge, TV consumer-savings expert and syndicated columnist at SavingsAngel.com

"With searing honesty, Lauren Greutman admitted that she and her husband sprinted after the illusive American dream and fell flat. She transformed herself into a renowned expert on frugal living who shares her knowledge and tips without scolding you."

—Valerie Rind, award-winning author of *Gold Diggers and Deadbeat Dads: True Stories of Friends, Family, and Financial Ruin*

"Lauren's personal experience with getting out of debt is truly inspiring. What's even more inspiring, though, is her willingness and ability to take what she's learned and to share it with others in the hope of helping them lead better, more financially secure lives."

—Sara Korab, Savings.com

"Lauren is a debt and frugal-living expert who makes personal finance engaging, exciting, and comprehensible to the masses. She is passionate about helping people get their finances in order, and her credibility is unquestioned given her firsthand, real-life money experiences."

—Andrew Schrage, Money Crashers

"Lauren Greutman has empowered millions of people to lead the best life possible on any budget. She is an incredibly savvy personal-finance expert with the refreshing ability to break down complex topics and make them accessible and fun. Her real-life experience of getting out of debt is inspirational and provides a road map for others that want to take control of their finances."

—Loren Bendele, cofounder of Savings.com and Favado

THE
RECOVERING SPENDER

THE
RECOVERING
SPENDER

How to Live a Happy, Fulfilled, Debt-Free Life

LAUREN GREUTMAN

CENTER
STREET

New York   Boston   Nashville

Center Street
Hachette Book Group
1290 Avenue of the Americas
New York, NY 10104
centerstreet.com
twitter.com/centerstreet

First Edition: September 2016

Center Street is a division of Hachette Book Group, Inc.
The Center Street name and logo are trademarks of Hachette Book Group, Inc.

The publisher is not responsible for websites (or their content) that are not owned by the publisher.

Library of Congress Control Number: 2016941408

ISBNs: 978-1-4555-9580-8 (trade paperback), 978-1-4555-9579-2 (ebook)

Printed in the United States of America

RRD-C

10 9 8 7 6 5 4 3 2 1

To my husband, Mark

You stood by me through this entire journey

and never gave up on me! You are such an

amazing husband, and I am so thankful for

your belief in me!

Contents

Introduction

I am a Recovering Spender. For years I struggled to balance a simple checkbook every month without bouncing a check. I found myself a young married woman, in over $40,000 worth of debt, with an underwater mortgage, running a $1,000 deficit every month. I tried computer spreadsheets, but they confused me. I much preferred pen and paper. I tried tracking my spending, but only felt defeated. For years, I read book after book and tried every personal finance system I could get my hands on, but with little success. There were some parts of any given system that spoke to me as a Spender, but I felt that most did not apply to me.

Through trial and error, I learned how to control my spending, and get out of debt once and for all. In the depths of my despair, I started to develop my own system, specifically for those of us who struggle with spending. It is meant to work for ordinary folks like me—and you.

If you are tired of creating budgets only to crash them, if you are sick of being broke all the time, or if you simply want to know how to start getting out of debt, then you are speaking my language. This book is not for savvy spenders who have it all together financially, are masters of their credit cards, and have robust Roth IRAs and stock portfolios. I am writing this book for *you*—the American Spender.

There is so much information out there for people who love learning about everything financial, but what about people like us? Where are the books for those of us who just can't seem to get it together? I wrote this book for the not-so-savvy spenders. The forgotten people when it comes to money management. We are the black sheep in the finance class, sitting in the back of the room slouched down with our heads hung low. We've gone through life thinking that we suck at math and there is something wrong with us. The ironic thing is that we want to get better, but we just aren't sure how to do it.

You may feel as if there's no hope because you've tried and failed and tried and failed again. The finance books aren't making a connection with what you need, instead they are making you feel depressed and helpless. "Just stop spending money," they say. Yeah, right. We both know things aren't as simple as all that, because we've tried and nothing worked!

Here's the good news: You don't have to be depressed and helpless anymore. I'm here to offer hope—because I've been there, found the answers, and made them work.

Somewhere along the road you may have been taught that you are not capable of handling your money, and I am here to tell you this is a *lie*! You were not born to be terrible with money, that is *not* who you are. Maybe you've tried to budget in the past, but failed. For years you've lain down and endured the pain because you didn't know there was a way out. Maybe all you really needed was someone to pick you up and help you see what is on the other side of the divide.

This book is the financial book for the person who doesn't enjoy talking about money. It is for the person who wants to learn how to get out of debt and stay out of debt once and for all. If you struggle to stop spending and have failed at budgeting many times in the past, this is the book for you! Let me be the one to pick you up, dust you off, and help you walk over that divide so you can see that there is hope on the other side.

I know what it takes to learn that the other side of the divide offers relief. I was a compulsive shopper for most of my life. My spending habits landed my husband and me under a mountain of debt. I would wake up most mornings and feel like there was a 400-pound weight on my chest. My spirit was crushed, the anxiety and stress were paralyzing, and I had no idea how to get out of the mess I had gotten us into.

What you'll find in this book is my story of how I found us buried in $40,000 of debt, and how I managed to dig us back out. I'll walk you through what it takes for a Spender to go into "recovery" with her spending, climb her way out of debt, and live a life of financial freedom.

I consider myself a Recovering Spender. I will always be a Spender and am always one decision away from falling back into my old habits. Through trial and error (okay, mostly error) I've found what works to keep me from spending money. I know what boundaries I need to keep in place, and what my trigger points are. I am a Recovering Spender, and I hope to help you get into recovery as well.

Throughout this book, I am going to share with you my struggles and weaknesses. I'll show you how someone like me can climb her way out of debt, learn how to happily stick to a budget, and start to take back control of her money and life.

I am not going to tell you that the process is a quick one, but you *will* get better. I have tried it all—the cheats, the quick fixes—but they all failed me. Why? Because I wasn't willing to do the hard work that it takes to get it done the right way, which is often the harder way.

In the second half of the book we will go through the Twelve Recovering Spender Steps you need to follow to get your life back. These are the steps I took to get my spending under control, successfully stick to a budget, and still have fun and enjoy life along the way. As someone who has been through this, I took the best parts of every program I've ever tried and created a new one using the things that worked best for me as a Spender. Consider this the "Official Spender's Guide to Recovery."

I am living proof that you can take back control of your spending habits and get yourself out of debt. Believe me, if I can do it, anyone can.

THE
RECOVERING SPENDER

PART
1

PART
1

Chapter 1

My Spending Addiction

It was the last day of June, which meant it was also the last day of my company's fiscal year. I put my ten-month-old son to bed a little early that night, because I had some serious work to do. I only had until midnight to reach my goal, a goal I had been working so hard for during the past eleven months.

I sat on my couch, staring at the brand-new laptop I had just purchased for my "business," my fingers flying over the keyboard. As the seconds passed and the clock ticked closer to midnight, my adrenaline pumped faster. I've always wanted to be successful and didn't care what it cost. I loved the recognition that my company offered me; it gave me a rush.

My mouth started watering as if I was about to bite into the best chocolate cake of my life. My blood was pumping…I couldn't fail this time, I had worked too hard for this. Was I really this close to success? I only needed fifteen more people to sign up and buy $200 worth of products, so I started making phone calls. I called multiple family members and friends, and the conversation went like this: "I am so close to my goal, would you mind signing up under me so I can place a $200 order for you? It won't cost you anything; I just really need to get to this goal tonight by midnight. It would mean the world to me." If they placed a $200 order, they were considered a new active team member, and I needed a certain number of active team members in order to qualify for my free car. I wanted to make it easy for them to join, so I covered the cost of their first order. I was helping them, and they were helping me. Every time they said yes, I took out my shiny new credit card and ran a $200 charge, plus an additional $30 for taxes and fees.

Most people would feel as if they were ruining their life, one charge at a time. I felt as though with every completed transaction my life was just beginning. I was exhilarated and excited about what was to come.

I ran my fingers across the numbers on the card and dreamt about what would happen when I told my team members that we had done it! We had become a top unit in the company. I couldn't let them down; we had all worked so hard to get to where we were today. It had been only ten months from the time I joined the MLM (multilevel marketing) home-based business to when I became a sales director, at the age of twenty-five. Only one month after that I had won a prestigious company car. We were setting records—or should I say they were helping me set records. Those records would propel me to the next level in my business and my life. Would I finally be able to live the life I always wanted? A life of luxury, where I could buy whatever I wanted, whenever I wanted it. The luxury I'd dreamt about since I was a little girl.

Growing up, my sisters and I loved to play MASH, a game popular among teens and tweens that "predicts" their future. You and a friend each take out a piece of paper and write the word *MASH* at the top of the paper, in big capital letters. *MASH* represents your home in the future. *M* means you'll live in a mansion, *A* means you'll live in an apartment, *S* means you'll live in a shack, and *H* means you'll live in a house. Then you both write a list of categories below your title, and three or four items under each category.

Our first category was always, "Who are you going to marry?" We typically chose two people we liked, and one who made us sick to our stomachs. It was always a good sign when you landed on a person you actually liked, not so good when you landed on the person you didn't like. My sisters and I would always scream when this happened, as if it really was predicting our future!

There was always a category about what car you would drive. I always listed the same four cars: a minivan, a limo, a Lamborghini, and a BMW. I guess I had expensive tastes from an early age. I don't think I even knew what a Lamborghini was, I just knew it was a luxury car, and I liked nice things.

The third category we typically chose was, "How many kids will you have?" I always chose low numbers for this category: 0, 1, 2, and 3 were favorites.

To get to the predictions, you start by choosing a number between 1 and 10 to use as a counter. Then you start counting through your choices, and when you reach your number, you cross the item off the one your pencil is on. You do this over and over again until there is only one item left in each category. The remaining items are considered to be your future.

I would play that game over and over again, and wish and pray that I would land on a mansion. I always wanted to live a life of luxury, hence the selection of cars I always placed in my car category. I have no idea where that desire for luxury came from, though, because my family wasn't one that put much value on it growing up.

But back to my big night building my business. I felt as if that dream of landing on the *M* in *MASH* was finally coming true.

My hands started to sweat. I repeated that conversation twenty times that night. Ten people said yes and signed up to help me. I had people underneath me who were signing their family members up too. And every time, I said, "Of course I'll cover the bill!"

Everyone was on board and it felt like a true family, all of us working together toward a common goal. I was on the phone with a superior team member, and we had calculators and notepads going, making sure that I was able to hit the goal I needed to hit to win the prize. Ten people left to go, ten more $200 orders left to charge. It was 11:30 p.m. I only had thirty more minutes to go. Orders were rushing in—five more to go, three more to go, last one in! *Done*, we did it! We made our goal with only minutes to spare! I had just won a prestigious car from my company and set a record for the person who won it the fastest in my region.

My good friend and coworker Sarah sat faithfully next to me the entire night, cheering me on. As soon as midnight hit and the deed was done, we rejoiced, popped open a bottle of champagne, and toasted my achievement! The bubbles of the champagne tasted like success. My face hurt from smiling so much. I had done it! I'd accomplished the seemingly impossible feat of winning a car after only being in the company for eleven months. This must be what success felt like.

My husband, Mark, sat on the side and watched all the commotion going on, happy that I was happy. He was a huge fan of mine, but he will tell you that despite his belief in me, he sat in the dining room that night with a sick feeling in his stomach, because he knew the damage I had just caused on that brand-new credit card. He was proud of me, but he could also see the future consequences of my actions. I saw nothing but success.

You would think that I would have noticed his worry. Looking back on it now, I think I was just too blinded by my excitement and the possibility of more success just ahead.

I paused a moment to dream of all of the praise that I would be getting the next month at our company seminar. The claps, the hugs, the questions of "How did you do it?" I knew this would be my year!

I had joined that home-based business company with a dream, a dream to live an independent life and bring home extra cash to help pay down debt. When I joined we were in credit card debt for the third time. I just couldn't seem to get my spending under control. We would get out of debt, then something would come up and we would fall right back into it again.

The truth is that by the time I received that "free" car, two months after I earned it, I was already in over $20,000 worth of debt—$12,000 from that last night of the month and another $8,000 in credit card debt. I was stuck in a vicious cycle, without the self-control to stop.

It was ironic that the same company I dreamed would help me get my spending under control and pay down debt actually made it worse. It was not the company's fault that I got into this mess. However, I do believe it plays a role in encouraging people to spend money they do not have on inventory to grow their businesses. I was a spending addict, and my addiction continued to get me into more and more trouble.

According to my calculations, I wouldn't get in too much more financial trouble and was safe for the month of June. After figuring all of my commissions, I had made more than $10,000 that month alone from the orders people under me had placed. That was a huge number, and I would be able to add that to my accolades whenever I was introduced at events. Life was good.

But I had one dirty little secret. During the month of June, I charged more than $12,000 to my brand-new credit card, much of it on the night of June 30 from signing people up to win my "free" car. In addition to covering the costs of people signing up, I had spent even more attending conferences, getting my nails done, buying new clothing for events, and many more frivolous purchases—everything that I thought made me look the part of a successful twenty-five-year-old businesswoman.

I told myself that everything would be all right because I had made $10,000. Paying $2,000 for this kind of success was what everyone does, right?

I had a few conversations with other people in my company, and they all agreed that this was what everyone did. People covered the costs in order to sign other people up under them all the time. It was considered an investment in their business and in their unit. Many people were encouraged to do this with the excuse that they pay themselves back with the commission bonuses that they received from hitting certain company milestones. The people encouraging them also got bonuses when they reached a new milestone, so they benefited as well.

After buying approximately $100,000 in product from the company for my customers, I was promoted to director. I was flown to new-director training in a fancy hotel in Dallas, where I was wined and dined and instructed in the art of making the sale.

Most of the women I spoke with at new director training were in the same boat as me, but in even more debt. My roommate at the training was in over $30,000 worth of debt from ordering products; her friend who was also there was in $45,000 worth of debt. The emphasis was always on achieving goals and success, not on how you actually got there. Dream big, they said, and you will achieve your goals.

The reality is that spending that much money in one night didn't faze me a bit. I wish I could say it had, but I did not care about putting us another $10,000 in debt. I already had a spending problem, proven time and time again by my uninhibited spending. Buying recognition made me feel good, and I was willing to spend thousands on it. I wanted it and never thought twice about the consequences. I was unfulfilled and empty and I needed recognition. The combination of those two things was a *disaster* for me.

I was definitely no stranger to dreaming big. I was always a dreamer and it was evident in everything I did. I grew up as a ballerina and was always a very hard worker. I would practice at home in my basement to perfection. My ballet studio, Ballet Regent, in my hometown of Saratoga Springs, New York, was the summer school for the New York City Ballet. My teachers were retired principal dancers from that company, so when the New York City Ballet came for its summer tour at Saratoga Performing Arts Center, they would dance with us at our studio. I danced with some of the best ballerinas in the world every summer until I was fifteen years old. I always loved being onstage and the center of attention. For some ballerinas, a solo onstage was terrifying, but to me it was my comfort zone. Looking back on old family VHS videos, I could see that this played out at home too. As the old images flicker by, you can often see me pushing my sisters aside to regain the spotlight.

I quit ballet at the age of fifteen because my teachers wanted me to move to New York City and study at the School of American Ballet. I knew that I would have to sacrifice so much to attend the school, and I was just starting to get to be a part of the "cool" group in junior high, which meant football games on Friday nights and much more social activity. I didn't want to miss out on life, so I eventually quit dancing and left it all behind.

I always had big plans for my life, and knew it would involve lots of money and "stuff." The problem was that I rarely thought my plans through, acting mostly on impulse based on what felt good at the time. No one could say that I failed in the "dream big" department; I just failed at thinking through what that would mean to everyone around me and my future.

It felt so good to be noticed for my success that not for one second did I stop and think I was a fraud and a fake. I assumed everyone did what I did, so no one needed to know that I had bought my way to the top. I eventually found comfort in that and ignored the nagging feeling of guilt inside. My guilt would bubble up a lot during my life of spending, but I'd gotten good at ignoring it and moving on.

I had been spending with abandon for years, often hiding my purchases in the trunk of the car so Mark wouldn't see them. I remember one time after I "won" my car when I had a shopping party at a local store with some consultants in my unit. The deal was that if I got six friends to go shopping with me at this store, we would all get 30 percent off our purchases that night.

I took full advantage of the 30 percent discount. After three hours of shopping, trying on every item of clothing in the store and staying until closing, I charged $600 to that same credit card, which now had more than $30,000 on it. When Mark asked what I had bought at the store that night, I told him I didn't buy much. What he didn't know was that I had more than $600 worth of clothing in the trunk of our car, which would stay there until he left for work the next day. I felt guilty, but that didn't keep me from doing the same thing over and over again.

That guilt had been there from the very start, when we got married at the young age of twenty-one. I was getting so used to the feeling that I didn't pay much attention anymore. The desire to spend became greater than the guilt I felt after. These spending habits started at a very early age and continued to haunt me for the rest of my teen and young adult life.

Chapter 2

The Value Switch

Winning that free car wasn't the first time I had made bad financial choices. I'd been making them throughout my teenage years as well, even though I was debt-free when I entered college at eighteen.

After I quit ballet when I was fifteen years old, I turned to playing field hockey in high school. I was recruited to play Division III field hockey at a few colleges. I chose to attend the State University of New York at Oswego. I was a hard worker, and would often stay after practice to run more or do more drills.

My parents paid my college tuition and sent me a weekly allowance. The allowance wasn't really enough money for me to live in the manner I desired, so to solve that little problem, I sold all of my college textbooks back to the bookstore right in the middle of the first semester. I earned a couple hundred dollars that provided the luxurious living I desired, but not the grades my parents expected. The first two semesters of my freshman year, I received a 2.4 and a 2.3 GPA. I was known for not going to classes and for partying too much at the bars. My desire to stay after field hockey practice and work harder started to decrease, and my coach started to notice. I was no longer a starting player in our games, and my grades started to drop significantly. Not surprisingly, it is hard to do well in school when you don't have any books to study.

Shortly after selling my books back to earn extra cash, I received a knock on the dorm room door from another student. He was participating in a fund-raising contest for a college group in which they raced to see how many people they could get to sign up for a specific credit card in a two-hour period. I filled out the form, with no real intent to use the card. I just wanted to help the guy out. A couple weeks later, I received that shiny new credit card in the mail, and suddenly my eyes were opened to all that was now available to me. I was hooked, and immediately started using it. I didn't have a car during my freshman year, so at first I was limited to using the card when I could hitch a ride with friends to the store. But once I brought a car back to school my sophomore year, I was playing with fire, and credit cards were the fuel. At any opportunity I would take the forty-five-minute drive to the nearest mall and shop my heart out, with no real plan on how I was going to pay the bill. It felt good, I looked fashionable, and I figured I would just pay it off in the summer when I went home to work at my waitressing job.

Early in that sophomore year, the same credit card company approached my field hockey team about doing a fund-raiser for our team. We were offered a certain amount of money per credit card sign-up, plus there was a bonus prize of $50 to $100 for the person who got the most people signed up. We all ran around campus getting students to sign up for credit cards, promising them they could just cut them up when they received them. One of my friends won the bonus prize for signing up the most people. She remembers that she was never paid the bonus and our team never received any money for the sign-ups. We had been scammed. The credit card company had won, and I had added another card to my name because of it.

I had no idea of the danger we were playing with back then, but we encouraged people to sign up and then cancel the cards. I wonder how many people actually canceled their brand-new credit cards after they showed up in their college mailboxes. I know that when I got my card it allowed me to continue to spend the way I wanted to; after all, I couldn't live like a broke college student!

Looking back, I see a common theme. I was a broke college student, I was a broke newlywed, I was a broke twenty-five-year-old up to my eyeballs in debt. Yet in all three situations I spent like I was a rich college student, a rich newlywed, and a rich twenty-five-year-old driving around in an Audi. Why? I wanted to appear as if I "had it all." When people talk about "keeping up with the Joneses," I wanted to be the Joneses. The thought of changing how I spent money was so overwhelming to me that it just didn't seem possible. I had no idea how to do it. It was too hard, I would tell myself. I felt that in order to get out of debt and learn how to spend money, I would have to totally retrain my DNA to stop it all. I had no idea where to even start, so I just continued to ignore it.

MY BIG SWITCH

Big changes had to happen in my life when we realized we were $40,000 in debt. *Big changes* that terrified me. It may seem strange, but the necessary spending changes I needed to make scared me more than continuing to live in a constant state of being broke. Many other Spenders that I interviewed also felt the same way; it is easier to just ignore it than to deal with it.

I had a big ah-ha moment one day when I was faced with a loss. In between the births of my first two children, I had a miscarriage. I suffered from infertility for about a year and a half after my miscarriage and struggled to make sense of what had happened. After multiple visits to the doctor and one surgery, we were finally able to conceive again. During that time of infertility, everyone around me was getting pregnant and having babies. I remember being so jealous and praying to be able to have more children. Right around the time of the miscarriage was when we had our big discussion about the debt I had racked up. Everything had come to a head at the same time, and I found myself slowly spiraling into depression.

I spent many days and nights weeping for more children. But I also worried that we might not be able to afford more kids. I find it no coincidence that these two big events happened around the same time. I had to take a serious look at my values again, and what I valued more than money was a family. I wanted a large family so badly that I was willing to make those *big* changes I'd been so terrified to make in the past. Resetting my values helped me realign my spending.

What are your values? Where do you spend your money? And do the two line up? If you are a Spender, my guess is that you've never sat down to define your values when it comes to money. I certainly never defined mine. I shopped impulsively and rarely thought of the consequences. I hardly even thought about what or why I was buying; it always just sort of happened.

I realized that I had a major value crisis going on in my life. My spending was not a reflection of my value system. I valued family, growing old together, education, safety, my faith, and togetherness. If you looked at my checking account, you would be fooled into thinking I really valued eating out for dinner, shopping, entertainment, housing, cars, and random "stuff."

My spending was putting my family at risk. I was hurting my marriage, my kids were not going to have any money to pay for a college education because I had no savings plan, I wasn't saving for retirement, and I had little sense of togetherness with Mark. I was thinking only about my own needs, and my selfishness was pushing me further and further away from the things I valued most.

I realized I *had* to make a change, not only for myself, but for my family. They needed a solid financial future, and I needed to stop spending money so I could give that to them. Sounds easy, right?

Suddenly I was faced with another hard decision. One of my values came from being a mom, and I didn't want to work full-time, but in order to get out of debt I saw no other option. I was struck with another value struggle that most finance experts don't even touch on. How could I be a stay-at-home mom, pay off my debt, and afford to live? This struggle affects us moms to the core.

Here's a scenario that may help explain this further:

The parents of two young children are facing the next steps in life, and many of their decisions are connected with household finance issues. With both parents working full-time, the family is on schedule to be completely debt-free in two years. But with two small children in preschool, the mother desperately wants to cut back on hours and stay home with her kids during those precious years. With more than $30,000 in debt and a tight budget, it is a difficult proposition. If she reduced her forty-hour workweek to ten hours, they could swing it. Their budget would be tight and they wouldn't be able to make any significant progress on their debts, but they could make it without any day care.

What price does one put on spending time with one's children in their early years? Is it even possible to assign a dollar amount to something like that? But because of financial pressures or lifestyle choices, many forgo this special time in order to better their current and future economic situation.

In the scenario above, there is no right answer. Spending more time with your kids now means delaying basically everything money-related: getting out of debt, saving for an emergency fund, retirement, college funds, and so on. Everything goes on the back burner for a few years. And there is no guarantee that the mother will be able to go back to work full-time once the children are in school. While that is certainly a steep price, millions would say it's worth it. Think of the shared memories created with children at this age. Think of the greater parental influence you might have—will it carry over into their later years? Who knows? In the grand scheme of life, these memories might mean having to work three more years before you retire, maybe more.

Other women choose to work in order to provide for their children and get them into a good school district. There is no right or wrong way to raise a family.

Amid all the great financial advice and articles out there, **remember that you have a life to live.** Why do we work? Why do we make money? Why do we want to retire? Why do we want security? These questions cut to the heart of life's meaning—and they underscore the roles that work and money play in our everyday lives. When mapping out your financial future, your end goal isn't simply a ton of money; it is comfort, security, and whatever makes you happy. Money is only a means to that end. But here's the rub—you're living right *now*.

Anyone could conceivably work sixteen hours a day, live in a tiny apartment for years, and never start a family. If you did this right out of college, you could probably retire at age thirty-five and never have to work another day. Would you even be living life? What do the kids say now—*YOLO*? "You only live once." That phrase usually alludes to an impending impulsive decision, but it also boils down to the fact that each of us has only one life to live.

This hits at the crux of what I am passionate about and why I wrote this book: the intersection of life and money. The whole point of becoming financially independent is the ability to live your life freely, without sacrificing your values.

Every big decision has financial consequences. I have made my fair share of decisions that bore horrible results and took me years to undo. Quite often, we need to make a financial choice that might hurt initially but is more than offset by the impact on the quality of our life and relationships.

Here are some examples from my own life:

February 2007: I had finally come to terms with my bad decisions. I stepped down from my position as a director with the MLM business, despite all of the debt we were in. My team was no longer meeting the required ordering needed, and I was suddenly faced with a $900-per-month lease payment to drive that "free" car. I added up all the debt we had and realized that with the failure of my formerly successful direct sales endeavor, we were now running a $1,000 deficit in our monthly budget and something had to give. I had only one option—I had to get a job outside the home. I went out that day and landed a job as a waitress at an upscale Ruth's Chris Steak House. But this meant being away from my son five nights a week. It was a decrease in quality of life, but it got us through a rough spot financially. I was willing to make a short-term sacrifice for a long-term gain.

Fast-forward to January 2008: I was working several nights a week and it had taken its toll on all of us. I wanted nothing more than to be a full-time mom. I just couldn't keep up with working anymore. Although we couldn't make much progress on paying down our debt, we decided that the benefit of having me at home with our two-year-old son was worth it.

We still had most of the debt, but we had to find a way to make life work on one income. Mark had a job opportunity that boosted his salary a bit, but our monthly budget was still short. I figured out that if we cut our grocery budget in half we could make it work. Thus began our introduction to the world of coupons.

June 2010–current day: I am debt-free. I work full-time on my website, while three of my kids are in school and the youngest is at Grandma's house a few mornings a week. I travel to New York City once or twice per month to go on the *Today* show, *Dr. Oz*, or another national TV program. I am a working mom, and I wouldn't have it any other way. I get to share my story of hope with millions of people every year, and for that I am incredibly thankful. My kids get to see our journey full circle, and they are proud of me and what I get to do.

There are many more examples of these significant life/finance choices that we all need to make. You need to figure out a way to make your value system the center of everything that you do. Then decisions become much easier to make, and you have more freedom than guilt in making them.

Paying off your debt or staying at home with your kids is a hard decision, but let me tell you that if you are a Spender you can make the choice right now to stop spending money and start paying attention to your finances.

I discovered that saving money is just as productive as earning it. If you go out and get a minimum-wage job that pays $150 per week, wouldn't it be the same as saving $150 per week? When you start to look at things this way, there is no reason why you can't have your cake and eat it too.

Over the next four years I learned how to save money and change my spending habits. It wasn't easy, but because what I was doing was aligned with my values, it was easier to find motivation and stick to it when times were hard. Our values are reflected in how we spend our money. Having money causes feelings of self-sufficiency and power; it touches everything. It is the very thing that makes life work.

I can't tell you what your values should be, but what I can tell you is that once your money and values are in sync, it is much easier to stop spending.

Chapter 3

Shoplifting and Credit Cards

When I was a teenager I had a problem with shoplifting. I wanted everything that I couldn't have, and because of my impulsive behavior and lack of self-control I would often find myself in trouble. I grew up in a middle-class home and had everything I needed. Yet I still craved more.

One day when shopping with friends at the mall, I went into my favorite clothing store and spotted an adorable outfit, but my mom had only given me enough money to buy lunch. I was just fourteen, so I didn't have a job yet. I remember thinking that maybe I could sneak some of that clothing out of the store without anyone knowing. I slipped on a pair of tight denim shorts, a white sparkly tank top, and a beautiful white-and-red-striped blouse. Then I put my regular clothing over them and walked out of the store. I couldn't believe it—I was so excited about what I had done. My friends and I bragged about it to each other, and the adrenaline surge of my success was exhilarating. I loved the rush of it all, especially the lack of consequences.

I came home and slipped my brand-new clothes into my closet, stuffed inside a large clothing box left over from Christmas. I pushed the box all the way to the back of my closet so that my mom wouldn't find it. I should have felt remorse, but I actually felt like I had just won the lottery! I started to do my homework, but I couldn't contain the rush of adrenaline that was flowing through my body. I could see myself doing it again and started to dream of all the new items I could take.

The next evening while I was in my room doing my homework, I heard my mother yell from downstairs, "Lauren, get down here right this minute!" It was that mom voice that says, "You are in the biggest trouble of your life."

I immediately wondered to myself, "How did she know?" Somewhere deep in my gut I knew that she had somehow found out about my trip to the store. I had no idea how, but she had. I came downstairs and one glance at her face told me I was in big trouble. She had her hands behind her back, which I thought was strange, but soon realized it was because she was holding the stolen clothing in clenched fists. She held up the clothes, tags dangling in the tense air. She had found them. And I was in deep trouble!

When writing this book, I realized I had never learned how she discovered the clothes, so I called her to ask. She said that she had been searching for something in my closet while I was at school and came across a strange box. She'd opened the box and knew instantly that I had stolen the clothes. I asked her how she knew they were stolen, and she said, "I knew they were stolen because many of your friends were stealing, you didn't have any money to buy them, and I certainly didn't buy them for you."

This was not the first time I had stolen. When I was fourteen I had started smoking cigarettes along with my older brother, Rick. One afternoon when out walking downtown, I tried to steal a pack of cigarettes from a local convenience store and got caught. The manager sat me down and gave me a stern talking-to, then let me go on my way. This time, with the stolen clothing, I had been caught by my mom, which made it even worse.

I am not sure if I had ever seen my mom so mad at me. It was as if she was one of those animated cartoon characters with smoke coming out of her ears. I wanted to escape into a dark hole and cry, and I wasn't sure what I was going to say to get myself out of trouble.

She asked me, "Lauren, did you steal from the mall yesterday?" Sweat started rolling down my brow. I lied and told her I had bought them for a friend, but she didn't believe me. I was trying not to make eye contact with her because the shame was so strong. I am a people pleaser, so having someone angry with me is almost as bad as getting attacked by a swarm of angry hornets. I tried to lie to her, but she was not having it. I felt as if my life was over.

To make matters worse, my mom made me pack up the clothing in a brown bubble mailer. I then had to write a letter to the store manager apologizing for the theft and explain why I did it, then mail it back to the store.

Mortified and embarrassed, I was banned from the store, my mom would not allow me to return to the mall, and I was grounded for a month.

Had I learned my lesson in greed yet? I wish I could say I had—but that was only the beginning of my spending addiction. The desire to spend was there and I just couldn't shake it.

THE WOLF AND THE KNIFE

Desire is such a powerful emotion that it makes you do unpredictable things. Have you heard of the folktale of how an Eskimo kills a wolf? He first coats his knife blade with animal blood and allows it to freeze. He repeats the process until the blade is completely covered in frozen blood. Then he fixes his knife in the ground with the blade sticking up.

The wolf smells something and, following his nose to the source of the scent, discovers the knife. He licks the blood-covered knife and is instantly pleased by the taste. He begins to lick faster and harder. Frantically, harder and harder the wolf licks the blade, until the blood is gone from the knife and he is licking a naked blade. He is so blinded by his desire for more blood that he does not notice as his tongue starts to bleed from being sliced by the blade. Because of his predatory appetite he desires more blood, not realizing that the blood he is craving is now his own. The Eskimo comes back in the morning and finds the wolf dead in the snow from his self-inflicted wound and the loss of blood.

Why share this story with you? We Spenders are like the wolf, and money is our knife. As a Spender, I would spend money and it would feel so good! It would give me a rush of adrenaline. I would then feel so guilty that I would get depressed. That depression led me to go shopping again. It was a vicious cycle that wouldn't end until I stopped doing it. The wolf wouldn't have died if it had stopped licking the knife and desiring more blood. The Spender will continue to inflict wounds on herself emotionally and financially until she learns how to manage her money and starts to take action to avoid the dangers that lie ahead.

I was used to making stupid financial decisions, but things got worse when the bad financial habits started to rub off on my husband. It's as if I was a wolf sharing that knife with her partner. I was helping him commit a slow suicide as well.

Just six months before I won my car that fateful night, my husband, Mark, was scouring Autotrader listings and the classifieds. He spent time at car dealerships, just checking things out. At that time we had two old and junky cars, but no car payments. Mark's car was a green 1994 Saturn. It was a standard transmission with no CD player and no air-conditioning, and he had to turn a crank to open the windows. It was so uncomfortable and embarrassing to drive. And it certainly wasn't the Lamborghini I had dreamt about as a child. He commuted to work forty-five minutes each way with his best friend, and whenever it was his turn to drive, his friend made it known how much he disapproved of Mark's car. After a while, it started to bother us both.

If Mark's car sounds bad, what I had to drive to my sales meetings was even worse—a 1998 red Ford Windstar with a huge dent and scrape on the back from when I had backed into a snowbank a few years earlier. I was embarrassed going to every meeting and sales event driving what we called "Big Red." I felt my peers would not respect me if I drove that hideous thing. I was humiliated and thought people were laughing behind my back. How was I to appear as a successful businesswoman who makes a lot of money if I drove this big red van to sales meetings? I thought my reputation was on the line, and I needed to protect that.

We didn't have any car loans and never had. We never once stopped to think about the fact that if we purchased a new car, we would have to get a loan for the first time. I thought that was what you had to do to get nice things. Everyone else did it, so it couldn't be a big deal. We had to have something nicer to drive. So that's when Mark began car hunting. It had to be a luxury-type vehicle that said, "This family is doing pretty well."

When Mark and I first started dating, he told me that his dream car was an Audi. When we started looking for a new car this time, I wanted my husband to have his dream. An Audi it was! It was January, and we had just been approved for a loan for $18,000 to buy a vehicle. We were both working full-time and had only one child. It was easy for us to find the extra $230 per month for that car payment. We found the car we wanted; it was about an hour and a half away in the city of Rochester, New York.

I remember the drive well—we were so excited! Our first *nice* car. We deserved this—we had worked so hard! Mark had a great job as an actuary and I was working full-time with my MLM home-based business and was a stay-at-home mom to our son, Andrew.

With Mark's parents watching our six-month-old son, we got in our red Ford Windstar and drove to pick up the car. When we got to the car dealership, we saw the car and it looked just as gleaming and beautiful as it had in the photos.

The sales guy asked us if we wanted to take it for a test drive, and we agreed, because that's what you're supposed to do, right? But truth be told, we were already sold. As long as it started and moved forward when I stepped on the gas, we were buying this vehicle with wood-trimmed dashboard, heated leather seats, and six-disc CD player. I sheepishly asked the guy if he would take less; he said he couldn't. He knew we were buying it; he could see it in our eyes and hear it in our voices—he had us. So we paid full price.

I remember how I felt driving it home—in a word, successful.

Looking back, I can see how I convinced myself that I needed this car, and how if I didn't get it I wouldn't be a success. Mark got his dream car and I got the car I needed in order to appear like a winner. My way of thinking changed drastically after this purchase, and not for the better. I drove around town in our hot car a little more proud, with my chin held a little higher. After all, I had a rear-windshield sunshade, so that our sleeping toddler would never get sun in his eyes. I drove a car all the moms wanted (or so I thought). That pride led to other bad financial decisions: buying things I couldn't afford and convincing myself that I would pay for them later. But later never came.

Fast-forward six months and we had just "won" the brand-new company car. I say "won" because technically it is a company lease and if you don't make a certain amount of sales in your team you have to pay them a co-pay to drive it. That co-pay can be up to $900 per month, something I wasn't aware of when I earned that dream car. The embarrassing Saturn and red minivan we had in our driveway were now replaced with an Audi and a luxury vehicle from my company. The total worth of our cars was now equal to the market price of our $65,000 home.

Had my values changed? If you asked me then, I would have said no. We went to the same church, lived good lives, and were great parents to our son. Those were the things that I valued in life. I was *not* a materialistic person. Or was I?

Chapter 4

The Image

I suppose I imagined that when other people saw my car they were impressed. It didn't occur to me that most people couldn't have cared less. It became extremely clear that my values had changed. What I wasn't clear about was how exactly I had gotten there.

I grew up in a large home, but certainly not a mansion by any stretch of the imagination. I had friends across town who had elevators in their homes and other costly luxuries, and there was always a shard of jealousy in my heart.

Saratoga Springs is a wealthy town, and I grew up knowing a lot of affluent people with expensive tastes. I knew what I liked and how I wanted to live my life. Looking back, I realize now that I had issues from a very young age with coveting what others had. I always wanted more stuff and would constantly compare what I had to others, to measure if I was keeping up.

Growing up, I remember giving many of my friends a tour of our home. I would lead them through all six bedrooms and three and a half bathrooms, and along the paths of seventeen acres of land, most of it beautifully landscaped by my mom, who was a master gardener. I would find myself thinking about how lucky they must think I was. This feeling continued into adulthood, often leading to my making purchases simply to keep up with others and fit in. I loved the feeling of having something that someone else didn't have; it made me feel special and gave me value.

Values are taught at an early age, and I am not sure where I was taught to value money and possessions the way I did. I don't remember my parents teaching it to me. They never wore flashy clothes or put much stock in appearances. We drove older cars and didn't travel much. Somewhere along the path of my life, I started to attach values to purchases and objects. When Mark and I got married, I never realized how ingrained this had become in my mind.

When our first holiday season came around, I knew I needed to decorate our apartment to make it feel warm and inviting for both of us. My family had always decorated for Christmas the day after Thanksgiving, and this was the first year I hadn't been home to help. I wanted to continue the tradition, so off I went to T.J. Maxx in search of the perfect two-foot Christmas tree.

When I walked into the apartment later that night, $200 more in debt, I felt as if I had just walked out of a fog. I had no idea what had just happened. How had everything just landed in my cart, and how had I used my credit card without being aware of it? I had only gone into the store for a Christmas tree, but everything else was just so cute! I came home with enough stuff to decorate our entire apartment.

Those surprise purchases that I would "accidentally" make kept on happening. Except I could no longer consider them accidents. I was keenly aware that I had a problem, but I had no idea how to fix it. There were moments of strength where I could say no and be so proud of myself, but there were many more moments of weakness.

Not surprisingly, our first arguments as a married couple were all about money. I would want to buy something that Mark felt was unnecessary. I started off our marriage as a Spender, and my problem would continue to get worse and worse until I hit my breaking point.

Three months after I earned the free car, we moved from our small starter home in upstate New York to Fort Mill, South Carolina. We had purchased a brand-new home on a whim while on vacation visiting Mark's brothers. They had moved to Fort Mill to be part of a ministry start-up, and we hadn't seen them in a while. We went to visit and left as home owners, purchasing a house just two houses down from the one his brother was renting. We had no intention of buying a house when we went to visit, and came home wondering what the heck we had just done. I was very good at making impulsive decisions, and Mark was easily swayed. It was a brand-new construction; we built it from the ground up. It was our dream house. We put zero percent down and had to go home and sell our house. There were at least a dozen times when I thought to myself, "What did we just do?" But we pressed on and moved forward with our decision. We sold our home in New York for $80,000 and moved to South Carolina into our brand-new $225,000 house.

Mark drove our Audi and I drove my brand-new luxury car straight through the night with my son sleeping in the back. All of our belongings were packed into a moving truck and driven down behind us. We had a dream, and we couldn't acknowledge that it—the American dream—was killing us! As we pulled into the driveway of our custom-built house, our debt was growing as high and fast as the weeds around our brand-new foundation. Our debt had now passed $40,000, but we still had our Audi and our free company car, and we looked as if we had it all, including a beautiful new house.

The stress of keeping up with the bills was giving me daily anxiety. Mark didn't know that we had so much debt, because I didn't tell him.

I figured it would only start a fight, and I was trying to take care of it on my own.

The stress became too much. Five months into living in our new house, while sitting on our plush couch inside our custom bedroom suite, I made the decision to start the money talk that would change everything. I knew I had to come clean with Mark about how much debt I had racked up. The secrets I had been keeping from him about my spending habits were getting too heavy to carry all on my own.

There were many days when the truth of how much debt I had gotten us in was on the tip of my tongue, but I couldn't bring myself to say anything. That afternoon, I sat on that couch crying, feeling the sting of guilt, regret, and fear. For a long time I had wanted to tell Mark, but I was afraid of his reaction and how resentful he might be. To make matters worse, we were already underwater on our mortgage in the home we had custom built just six short months before. Our builder went bankrupt halfway through completing our development, and our neighborhood was left in shambles, with half-built houses, construction debris, and lost hopes. The thrill of owning a huge home was over, and the reality of our dangerous situation was starting to kick in.

THE CONFESSION

I called Mark up into our master bedroom after Andrew was put down for bed that night. Mark was working remotely from home at that time for the same actuarial company that he worked for when we lived in New York. He walked into the room not expecting what I was about to tell him.

I finally blurted out, "Can we take equity out of our home?" I thought to myself, "Oh no, I can't turn back now. I have to do it. I am so scared. Will he leave me? Will he be so mad he can't forgive me?"

What I didn't know was that Mark knew what I was about to confess, but was in denial. He knew we had credit card balances, but he didn't know the full extent. My day of reckoning had come, and I had to tell him. I just couldn't hide any longer.

I laid out all of our credit card statements on our bed and told him everything. For the previous four years I had been spending money with reckless abandon. Those shiny plastic cards were just too much fun to play with. I had lost all self-control and ability to say no to my shopping desires.

I would wake up at night and cry, I was so ashamed about how I had handled our money. I was trying to manage the bills and keep the truth from Mark, so he didn't know how bad it had gotten. I had hidden the last of our credit cards from him; he didn't know we had over $40,000 in overdue debt. I was so full of shame for not telling him about the cards, and despite his calm and forgiving demeanor, I was terrified to tell the truth out of fear of his anger and disappointment. Mark was also too afraid to ask me how much in debt we were. The problem was that because we weren't talking about it, the debt kept on growing. We both knew it was going on, but we ignored it. We were in the depths of denial.

We had gotten to the point where if we didn't have enough money to pay all of our monthly bills, I would ignore one bill to be able to pay off another. Then the next month I would do it all over again, juggling all the bills so that our utilities stayed on. And I did all of this while sitting in our large, expensive custom home that was slowly draining us of every single penny.

What could we do to get ourselves out of this mess? We had been in and out of debt so many times, and I was so sick of it. I wanted to be out of it for good this time, but I had no idea how to make it stick and not plunge right back in again.

I had tried to stop spending cold turkey in the past. But one trip to Target and my goal of no spending would be forgotten. Coming home with a car full of beautiful home-decor pieces made me so happy that I couldn't grasp the damage I had done until the adrenaline rush had worn off. Then the guilt of what I felt was unbearable, and I would start spending again.

I started to realize that spending wasn't my real problem, but more a symptom of a larger one. I realized that while I valued certain things, my spending was not a reflection of those values.

Money, life, and heart are inexorably linked, and I was missing the bigger picture. I could not separate my household finances from everyday social interactions, work habits, and my heart and mind. I sat down and thought about that for a while one day, realizing that in order to get out of debt, I needed to change the way I thought. I needed a mind-set shift, one that didn't involve being mad at Mark because he was making me stick to a budget or not giving me cash to spend.

This is a hard thing for a Spender to grasp. We Spenders usually only see the things that we want, and fail to see how our purchases are affecting others, and we tend to be very impulsive. Once I started to see how my spending was affecting my family, I was able to start making small changes. It was a slow process that required a lot of work and mistakes. It certainly didn't happen overnight, and there were many more times I messed up and got us into even more trouble.

There were many times when a situation would come up out of the blue as a reminder of my past, and I had major decisions to make. Would I fall back into my old spending habits, or would I stay strong and press on? For example, one day I received a large manila envelope in the mail.

Upon opening it I saw that I was being audited for my business two years prior. The letter said that I needed to pay the IRS $17,000 in the next thirty days, because they were disallowing all of my deductions from that business. I called Mark in a panic; not only was I thirty-four weeks pregnant with my second child, but we were finally making progress on paying down debts and sticking to a budget. This was a sucker punch, and I felt myself wanting to shop to deal with the stress.

I called my accountant, and after a nice pep talk from him, we appealed the audit. After a year of going through deductions and having meetings with the IRS, we got the amount down to only $2,500. Owing that instead of $17,000 was a huge relief. But we were still in a lot of credit card debt and now we owed the government another $2,500 we didn't have. Thankfully we were able to borrow money from family members, with the hope of paying them back quickly.

If being $40,000 in debt, underwater in our mortgage, and running a $1,000-a-month deficit wasn't enough, I now had to figure out how to get out of debt and stay that way. In order to change the way I managed and viewed money, I had to make some major lifestyle changes.

I was so sick and tired of being broke. I had gotten to the point where the pain of staying in debt was greater than the uncomfortable (and sometimes painful) changes that I needed to make in order to get us out. **When the pain of staying in debt is greater than the pain of changing your spending habits, *then* you will make the changes needed to get out of debt.**

If you are a spending addict, you may have told yourself, as I did, that you have the self-control to stop spending money and the ability to stick to a budget when you want to. You may even succeed for a month. But then one bad financial decision pushes you over the edge again. You have to come to a point where the pain of staying broke is greater than the pain of stopping to think about the way you spend money.

I needed to come to grips with that. Did I want to be broke and stressed my entire life? Or was I okay with making some hard decisions and changing for good this time? Could I take that same passion that I had when dancing as a child and turn it toward a passion for being debt-free? Could I harness that good work ethic I used when winning that prestigious car and put it toward getting out of debt? I had some strong character traits that could help me get out of debt, but I needed to start using them to be able to conquer this debt monster.

I realized that in order to get my spending back under control and get out of debt, I needed to take a stand for the principles that guided my everyday life, and make my spending a reflection of what I truly valued. Once I realized that, and set up some strict boundaries for myself, everything started to change for the better. It was a slow change requiring constant boundary setting, but it is possible to be a Recovering Spender.

After all, I am the living proof.

Chapter 5

How Disagreements over Money Saved Our Marriage

After realizing that my values had to change dramatically, I knew I had to continue working on my marriage. Things were becoming more difficult for us. Not that we were heading for divorce, but we had been arguing a lot more than usual.

Study after study says that money is the number one cause of divorce in America. But is money truly the cause of most divorces, or are there underlying issues that are covered up by using money as a scapegoat? I married a Saver; I am a Spender. I had no idea this was the case when we first got married, and here we were seven years later, deep in debt. During our marriage we've experienced many ups and downs. Many of these have been about money, but looking back, the money issues actually grew from much deeper ones. I think our money fights and dealing with so much debt and stress actually saved our marriage, because we were finally confronting our problems head-on. Deeper issues were there from the start.

IT ISN'T MONEY, REALLY, THAT PEOPLE ARE ARGUING ABOUT

I can remember when Mark and I were in that big financial pit. I took the blame because the vast majority of our credit card debt came from me. Mark remembers knowing that all of this debt existed, that it wasn't his fault, and that there was nothing he could do about it. We had some pretty heated fights. If we had participated in one of those marriage/divorce studies, our disagreements would certainly had fallen under the financial category.

But dig deeper and it is clear it wasn't money that we were fighting over. Behind his back, I had racked up a bunch of debt. And before I knew it, we were in a mess—the kind of mess that has the potential to rip families apart. Deceit, fear, spending addiction, distrust—these were the underlying issues in our marriage—and they existed before the credit card debt. "Disagreements over money" was more a symptom than a cause of our problems. We were forced to work through some deep issues. It was hard, and it took time. But at the end of it, those "disagreements over money" might have saved our marriage.

Have you ever sat down and thought about what money actually is? You work at your job and get paid money. You go to the store and buy food using money. You use money to pay for the house you live in. So right off the bat, I've covered work, food, and shelter—the basics of living. But wait, there's more—you use money for health care, to provide for your retirement, to give to charity, to buy anything and everything. Money enables us to live.

If a couple is constantly disagreeing about money, then they are disagreeing about the very things their relationship and lives are based on.

MONEY AS THE PROBLEM IS TOO SIMPLISTIC

It might seem that if you just stop arguing about money then all will be good, and that if you simply had more money, you wouldn't need to argue about it.

Why then do we see so many wealthy couples filing for divorce? Why do we see so many families scraping by who have amazing marriages? The answer is that money is not the real issue. It merely covers over much larger issues beneath the surface.

More families are struggling and living paycheck-to-paycheck than ever before. Mark and I were there, and many of our best friends are living this way. And I bet that even if you're not there now, you are still familiar with living on the financial brink. And as far as a marriage is concerned, struggling financially can really strain everything. But it doesn't have to.

For any given struggle, you can use it as a source of strength, or it can destroy you. I know there can be issues in any marriage regardless of financial means, but I also know of many super-strong crazy-in-love couples who are just barely getting by.

Here's my take on this (and it comes from my own experience)—when you don't have enough money, you are forced to make decisions together, good or bad. Financial hardships force you to come together and decide the priorities of your family and then put your money to those ends. It forces frugality. One of my favorite all-time quotes is from the Roman philosopher Cicero: "Frugality includes all the other virtues." That just sums it up perfectly, right? When you decide to spend less money and make life work, good decisions impacting all areas of life will follow.

OUR STORY

I met Mark as a sophomore at college in upstate New York. I was from Saratoga Springs, a town known for its Thoroughbred racetrack, white-pillared mansions, and upscale boutiques lining Broadway. Everywhere I looked, money offered the promise of "the good life" and everything that went along with it. Mark's smaller hometown was worlds away from the Saratoga lifestyle I saw growing up. He was from New York's proverbial rust belt, where major businesses have moved away, leaving high unemployment rates, closed shops along Bridge Street, and a largely blue-collar population. But it's also a place where people know the value of a dollar, love their hometown, and continually work to revive their community.

The state school I attended was my college of choice for three important reasons: the criminal justice program was strong, and this was my major; I had been recruited for the field hockey team; and my parents had gone there as well. Little did I know that my decision to attend this school would be the best one of my life.

The summer between my sophomore and junior years I decided to stay at college rather than go home. I had a job bartending, and worked with the college theater program. I was learning to love the town of Oswego, with its annual summer festival, including three days of music, food, and bands playing into the night along the shores of Lake Ontario. Life was simpler there than back home, and I enjoyed it. Most of all, I was falling in love with a guy I saw playing drums in my church, a talented guy I'd heard about from his sister, who was in the youth group I led.

While I was nicknamed "the Princess" by my family for my uptown tastes and somewhat lazy ways, Mark was truly a prince—hardworking, academically gifted, attending college on a scholarship in economics and math, and a musician who loved drums and the rock group Rush. He valued family, wanted to make his parents proud of his achievements, and saw education as a way to move up in the world and better his life.

Then I came along. It's significant that we met in church, for despite some outward differences of background and geography, our Christian faith was and still is our first priority. It's what brought us together, what binds us together, and what forms the foundation of our lives on a daily basis.

Even though I came from a wealthy town, my family and Mark's were more similar than one might guess. My parents were hardworking. My dad was first a schoolteacher and was later employed by General Electric. He and my mom built our home together. I grew up with a mother who knew the value of money. She knew how to budget, was careful with what she saved and spent, and also knew how to give generously. She also loved bargain hunting, and taught me the tricks of finding the best deals. Whenever we went shopping, we always checked the clearance racks first, and rarely paid full price for anything. My father's work ethic, very much like Mark's and his father's, was ingrained in me from my earliest years. It took me a long time to realize that I was smart and a hard worker. It wasn't until I met Mark, who challenged me in many ways I never had been challenged before, that I realized my full potential.

My parents provided all the necessities. I always knew that if I wanted something unnecessary and expensive, like a designer purse, I had to work for it. From the age of sixteen, I was busing tables and working in local shops to afford those purchases. I never wanted to go without the things I dreamed about, even from an early age.

Mark came from a family of similar values. His father owned an upholstery business, and his mother, who had a master's degree in education, chose to stay home and raise her four children. While Mark never went without, he knew from an early age that if he wanted any-thing extra—toys or a bike—he'd have to work and save for it. His fam-ily never used credit cards and taught him to live frugally. At the age of nine he had a paper route, and he used that money to buy the things he wanted. In high school he was given $100 a year for clothes. If he wanted anything beyond that, he had to work and pay for it himself. This habit stayed with him in college, where he worked summers building swimming pools to earn spending money, and bought his first car with cash (a for-eign idea to me at the time)—a rusty used Nissan Stanza that was prac-tically falling apart. Education was important in his family. He studied hard, earned excellent grades, and received an academic scholarship to college.

He had his dreams, like driving the Audi we would eventually buy, and maybe living in a high-rise apartment in New York City. But he never expected to get those things without hard work and thrift. He lived according to those values growing up and into college. He was on track to make a good life for himself, and had no thoughts of marriage when we met, telling me that he didn't want a wedding until he was forty. He assumed it would take time to build a career and a solid savings account.

Then we started to hang out a lot. From the minute I laid eyes on him playing the drums at our church, I found myself falling in love. I had dated enough jocks and jerks in high school to know that this guy was different—quiet, considerate, studious, serious, and of course handsome!

Mark first asked me out on a date in the parking lot of our favorite park overlooking the vast waters of Lake Ontario. We had hung out at a friend's house that night, and I knew he liked me when he started holding my hand under the blanket while we were watching a movie. After the movie was over, he drove me to the parking lot where my car was parked, and said, "So, will you go out on a date with me?" The butterflies in my stomach were fluttering so hard, I felt I might throw up. I said yes, and we decided to go out the next night.

There we were, in an Olive Garden, the place where broke twenty-somethings go for a romantic date. You can't beat the never-ending salad bar and breadsticks! We had a great night talking about each other's families, our pasts, and our future life goals. The check came to the table and Mark said, "Shoot, I forgot my wallet!" I ended up paying for dinner that night, on our first date, on a credit card. This was one small precursor of the financial mistakes to come. Mark was very laid-back and didn't give much thought to details. It was a great character trait, one that I loved about him, but his lack of attention to detail would eventually become something in our relationship that I would take advantage of. It was easy to spend money knowing that he wasn't looking at our bills and accounts.

Mark went back to college in late August after our summer of falling in love. We knew we wanted to get married and talked about it often. We lived three hours apart and spent many late nights on the phone chatting about what our future together looked like. I visited him at his college frequently, horrified to find nothing more than frozen pizzas in the freezer and some ramen noodles in the cupboard. I spent much of our time on those weekends filling up his pantry, then taking him out to dinner. He was too cheap to care about what he was eating. He could eat the same three things every day and never get sick of them.

After six months of dating, he asked me to marry him on New Year's Eve at midnight—right after the fireworks started going off in "our" park. I should tell you that to buy my engagement and wedding rings, Mark sold his beloved drum set on eBay. And it was just the first of many sacrifices he made for me.

We started making wedding plans, although many people tried to discourage us from moving forward too quickly, saying that at twenty we were too young to be engaged.

But we quickly started premarital counseling with our pastor, wanting to be prepared for a lifetime commitment. We talked about children, faith, forgiveness, and our goals in life. We *never* talked about money. We never talked about how we handled money or what our money goals were. During that time, I had no idea it would be an issue. I had no idea we were so different with our money. I just thought Mark was broke all the time, and that since I was making more money as a bartender I could spend more. I never once saw Mark as a Saver, and myself as a Spender. I can look back at that time and wonder if things would have been different had that been discussed in our counseling sessions.

My parents paid for our wedding, and I didn't have to lift a finger. I was very budget-conscious, because my parents were footing the bill, and I chose a simple, strapless $300 wedding gown with a long veil that cost as much as the dress. I wore long white gloves and a family heirloom pearl necklace. I didn't think much about anything that summer we got married. All I knew was that we were so in love and wanted to be together forever. We had only known each other for thirteen months prior to saying, "I do." Some would say it was a recipe for disaster, but we knew it was a fairy tale.

I remember one of our first arguments was over a bag of Doritos. On our first grocery store outing as a married couple, Mark was shocked when I tossed a full-price bag of Doritos into the cart. He couldn't believe I was so casual about buying a $4 bag of chips, something he never allowed himself. "What are you doing?" he blurted. I remember staring at him like he was crazy. I wanted Doritos, so why did he care? He also found it odd that I insisted upon wheeling the cart up and down every aisle, with no shopping list or plan about what to buy—just picking and choosing as I walked along. It was then I discovered that Mark bought about six items a week, and knew exactly where they were in the store. That was no way for a princess to eat, so I got my Doritos despite his disapproval. Looking back, we can laugh about that now, yet in some ways it was a tiny but important blip on a radar screen that we ignored. We never realized we handled money so differently and how huge a role this issue would play in our relationship and future.

After we were married, we moved into our first apartment, on an upper floor in a junky old house painted half white and half teal green. It was an ugly house and was flea-infested, but it was our first place together as husband and wife. We paid $325 per month and all of our furniture was hand-me-downs. Thoughts about how to live never concerned us. We were together. We were young and full of dreams and energy. Anything was possible. And we didn't need much apart from each other. Or so we thought. Our wedding gift money kept us afloat for a while, as well as income from odd jobs. Mark tutored, I worked at a winery, and we were getting by. When we needed or wanted things out of reach of our cash flow, we found it easy to charge them on credit cards—or I should say, I found it easy. Mark was not quite on board with the credit card life yet.

Mark finished out his last year at the State University of New York at Fredonia to graduate magna cum laude with a double degree in math and economics, with a wife, and Doritos in the cupboard. Following his graduation, we moved back to his hometown. We had a pug named Maddie, and since we couldn't find a decent rental place that allowed dogs, we purchased a small starter home with the help of a $5,000 loan from his grandma Rose. Since Mark had been such an excellent student in college, he got a job as an actuary immediately after graduation. Credit was not hard to come by with his job and income. Even though we had no idea how to handle credit cards, loans, budgets, or to plan for the next year, let alone next month, we were offered credit and loans at every turn.

Chapter 6

Spenders versus Savers

Three years into our marriage I started working with the MLM cosmetics company, and as I shared in chapter 1, it didn't go well. Mark and I still had never really sat down and made a budget or talked about our money personalities. Arguing about my spending had become sort of a habit. I thought Mark was too cheap and never felt I was doing anything wrong.

Spending habits can be a reflection of so many other personality traits. Impulsive people tend to spend more money, whereas hesitant people tend to be tightwads. The tightwad typically spends less than he would like to, because he just can't make up his mind. Spenders enjoy spending money, but have none left over because they spend it all. When the two types come together in a marriage, it seems as though the "opposites attract" theory should make it work, but it does not. The tightwad likes to save money, but gets frustrated because the Spender is always spending their savings. The Spender gets mad at the tightwad because he "never likes to have fun" and spends the money despite the partner's wishes. It continues as a source of contention. This is exactly where Mark and I were stuck, in the endless cycle of spending, saving, spending, saving. Then it turned into anger, resentment, ignoring, fighting... and on and on.

IF YOUR SIGNIFICANT OTHER IS A SPENDER, HOW DO YOU HELP HER?

If your significant other is a Spender, you can help her, but you have to be careful with what you say. I recently sent out a survey to over 70,000 people on the e-mail list of my website, laurengreutman.com. I got over 2,200 responses in twenty-four hours. These 2,200 Spenders say that among the reasons they spend money are depression, anxiety, and lack of self-control. I can tell you from experience: When you are talking with a Spender, she may already feel terrible about her spending, but she may have no idea how to control it. Start by offering to sit down and pay your bills and budget together. When Mark and I finally did so, it took such a heavy weight off of me.

HOW A MONTHLY MEETING SAVED OUR MARRIAGE AND MONEY

One thing that a Spender will need every month is a budget meeting. Why? Spenders usually have a good pulse on the household monthly needs. When you are a Spender, it's not as if you can just quit buying things. You need things like food, gas, and toilet paper. It is very important that the Spender has support, encouragement, and a sense of responsibility to the process. Taking away her money, giving her an allowance, or changing all the passwords on your computer will not cure the problem. She needs to feel a sense of entitlement and participation in the process. A Spender will often feel like a teenager if you take the budget away and give her an allowance. She will not feel empowered, which may turn into resentment and then into more spending.

At our monthly budget meeting we sit down with an agenda. Our goal is to work *together* to plan out the month before it happens. Mark is the one taking care of the monthly bills and organizing the month using a budgeting program that we created. I am the one who has my finger on the pulse of what is going on with the family. I typically know what birthday parties we have to attend, how much I need for groceries, and other family needs. When we work together, we actually budget successfully. If one piece is missing, the budget falls apart for the month. In this instance, our differences with money are actually a blessing, because they complement each other. Because I am a Spender, I know where I have to spend money. Since Mark is a tightwad, he prefers spreadsheets and numbers. It works amazingly well, but only because we are both on board.

When I have my monthly budget meeting with Mark, I feel as if I have only one job for the month—to stay within the boundaries of our budget.

I like the challenge of getting our budget as low as possible. If we need sneakers for our kids, I love to research the best deals and find them for less. I learned how to negotiate our phone bills, save money on gas, and so much more. There are many ways that I learned how to scrimp and save over the years, and I thoroughly enjoy the challenge. Being a part of the budget gives me a sense of ownership over the process, because I helped create the plan. I was given a voice, instead of just being given an allowance (which is a common way people try to deal with Spenders). I now have myself to blame if I overspend, because we discussed everything before it even happened. I had my opportunity to provide insight on how I wanted to spend our money that month, so I have to take responsibility for my overspending, which was very hard for me at first. I know that I have the opportunity at the beginning of every month to decide how much I want to spend on clothing. If I exceed my budget, it is because of my lack of self-control and discipline.

Did the ability to take responsibility come easily? Heck no! It took many months of screwing up, and going to Mark to confess my over-spending so he could rearrange the budget without any bounced checks. I would come to him with my head hanging low, feeling ashamed that I couldn't stay within our budget.

There were many times when I would spend our grocery budget on clothing purchases or activities out with my moms' group with the kids. It was hard for me to say no to time spent shopping at the mall with friends, and lunch and play dates at expensive kids' museums. Instead of saying no, I would use our grocery money on these activities and try to eat from the pantry instead. This would leave us with nothing to eat, forcing us to eat out at a restaurant and go over our budget.

I started to doubt my ability to stop spending money and stick to a budget. I felt as if I could never get it together. You may have felt the same way, that you've tried many, many times to get your spending under con-trol but it just never stuck. There is hope for you, and it comes during the monthly budget meeting.

An important part of this budget meeting is that the tightwad doesn't freak out on the Spender. You must realize it is a process and that it will take a few months to get the right numbers and ability to make it come together. If you are a Saver, be patient, continue to work together to get the budget back on track, and continue to encourage the Spender.

IF YOU ARE THE TIGHTWAD READING THIS BOOK, I HAVE A MESSAGE FOR YOU

Spenders typically feel bad about how they spend their money. Tell-ing them how horrible they are with money doesn't help the situation—it only makes it worse. By giving them a set amount of money as a punishment, or changing all of your Internet passwords around Christmastime, you are just delaying the inevitable crash of the Spender. You need to work together, even though you don't understand each other's spending habits, and learn how to complement each other. That being said, you need to find any opportunity to praise the Spender when she makes a good financial decision. You need to encourage, offer forgiveness when mistakes occur, and give praise when there is a job well done. Just to clarify, we are talking about someone who wants to get better and stop spending money, not a person who has a total disregard for how you feel. A Spender who doesn't want to stop spending money has a different story from mine, and I assume that because you picked up this book, you are ready for a change.

When I first sat down and blurted out to Mark that we were in $40,000 worth of debt, I expected him to yell, cry, or just walk out of the room. His reaction was exactly what I needed in order to start the recovery process. He said, "I forgive you. Let's get out of this together." I cried tears of joy that day, tears of relief. My secret was out, and it didn't ruin me as I thought it would. Those words allowed me to have the confidence to heal and move forward. I shudder to think what would have happened if he had said, "Yeah, right, you've been like this forever, and I don't know how you are going to fix this." I look back on his reaction, and believe his support was the main reason I was able to have the confidence to start on my path to recovery.

His forgiveness gave me confidence that I could change, just like he gave me the confidence that I was smart earlier in our relationship. It helped me get started on the right path. Give your Spender the confidence that she can do this, too! You are on the same team.

NOW LET ME TALK TO THE SPENDER

As a Spender, you need to allow the tightwad in your life to have some say in the way you spend your money. That conversation should come up every month in your monthly budget meeting. As a Spender, you may need to stretch yourself and think about how the tightwad may be feeling. Mark always felt he had no control over our money, because I would spend it before he could even touch it. He had dreams and visions of what he wanted our retirement and lifestyle to look like, but they were crushed when I got us into so much debt. To make matters worse, I wouldn't tell him and he wouldn't ask about my spending, and when he did ask there was always an argument. I would feel as if he was trying to control my money (even though I felt out of control).

You may feel defensive at first, but remember that the tightwad in your life really wants the best for you and your future. I know that for me it helps to check things over with Mark, because that keeps me from being impulsive.

Being impulsive is a character trait that Spenders in my survey reported also feeling. It is something that I am constantly having to deal with. There were many times when I didn't check with Mark before making a purchase and acted on impulse. I once came home with a pug puppy because I impulsively bought her. These impulse purchases would cost me thousands of dollars. If I had checked it over with Mark, I wouldn't have made those mistakes.

When we first started learning how to work together with our money, I went to him even though I didn't want to. Why? Because I made a commitment to him and to our future. With every purchase decision I made, I checked it over with Mark. I wanted to make sure I wasn't acting rashly and that he agreed with the purchase. This meant I had to learn to stay out of certain stores, because they were a huge temptation for me to overspend.

In one conversation after that fateful evening talking about our credit card bills, I remember giving him permission to tell me when I was making a bad financial decision. If you are a Spender and you want to change, you need to give one person the power to say something to you about it. It is not comfortable, but Mark's willingness to tell me when I am making a bad decision has helped me realize what my triggers are and how to stop my spending in its tracks.

HOW TO STOP FIGHTING ABOUT MONEY

Just stop fighting about it and everything will be fixed. Seems like an easy solution, right? I am not sure anything could be further from the truth. A recent study by Jeffrey Dew and colleagues, "Examining the Relationships Between Financial Issues and Divorce," published in the journal *Family Relations* in 2012, found that people associate money with deeply held meanings, feelings of self-sufficiency and autonomy. And because people associate their views about money with these feelings, fights about money aren't really about money at all. They are often about those deeply held meanings, and therefore they last longer and are more intense when money is the topic of discussion.

Our marriage was in trouble. From the outside it could have looked as though it was all because of our financial struggles. The truth was, we were broke, but in a real way, not a monetary way. A way that could have led to divorce down the road. But because we learned how to communicate about our money in a way that was healthy, we saved our marriage.

Chapter 7

How Differences in Upbringing Affect Your Marriage and Money

Growing up, I had friends who were rich and friends who were poor. I myself grew up in the middle class, so the lifestyle I was accustomed to had a certain set of rules. In her book *A Framework for Understanding Poverty*, Ruby K. Payne, Ph.D., suggests that there are three classes in America: the poverty class, the middle class, and the wealthy class. Dr. Payne writes about how each class has its own set of hidden rules. Hidden rules that are a part of your environment are learned by being raised in that environment, and being taught by role models in that environment.

Payne states that the hidden rules when it comes to money are very different depending on the class you are raised in. If you are raised in the poverty class, money is meant to be used and spent; you often give money away to someone else who needs it more. You also may spend your money more freely than someone in the middle or wealthy classes.

If you were raised in the middle class, money is meant to be managed. You may have grown up knowing what a budget is, how to put money in a savings account, and how to save for things that you want in the future.

The wealthy class thinks money should to be conserved and invested for future generations. If you grew up knowing what a trust fund was, you are probably a part of this class.

With that information in mind, let's look at the following scenario:

Joey is a smart boy who lives in a small town in Maine with his elderly grandmother. Joey always wanted to do better in school, but when he brought his homework home he had no one to help him. He had to figure out how to do it on his own, so he struggled in school despite being very smart. When Joey reached sixth grade he had a teacher who recognized his talent but realized he lacked the support at home. His teacher, Mr. Singer, worked hard with Joey that year and got him a scholarship to an afterschool electronics program. Mr. Singer formed a bond with Joey, and since Joey didn't have a father they became very close. Mr. Singer helped him throughout middle and high school, and literally changed his life. Joey was always very intelligent, and now with confidence in his abilities he graduated with honors and got a full ride to the college of his dreams. He worked hard in the engineering program and graduated with a degree to become an electrical engineer. He fell in love and married a beautiful woman named Emma, who came from a family of schoolteachers and wanted to help students in poverty. Since Joey came from poverty, they had a lot in common.

But shortly after their marriage began, they realized that they had different philosophies when it came to raising a family and money. Joey would often buy on a whim, not consulting with Emma when making large purchases. He would often give their money away to family members who didn't work or try to make their own living. Emma constantly tried to sit down and make a budget with him, but he could never stick to it. Emma fears for their financial future because Joey has already racked up over $15,000 worth of credit card debt, buys things instead of paying the bills, and has no idea how to budget. Joey doesn't understand why Emma gets so upset when he buys things for the kids. He didn't have much growing up and he wants his kids to have more than he did.

If this sounds familiar to you, then you are in the middle of a money-class struggle. Joey was raised in the poverty class and Emma was raised in the middle class. Joey learned that money is meant to be used and spent; when his family got money when he was growing up, they went out to eat, bought a video game, or bought something else they could never afford. His family rarely had money, so when they had it, they spent it.

Emma was raised with the lessons that money needed to be managed. Her parents had her open a savings account when she was twelve, and she learned from them about saving for a rainy day.

Both Joey's and Emma's families' hidden rules are strongly ingrained in them, so much so that they have no idea how to make their relationship work anymore. Before they surrender and file for divorce, they need to think about this: Her normal is not his normal. In order for him to change, he needs to be surrounded by people in the middle class and want to learn the language that Emma speaks. He needs to start understanding the hidden rules of the middle class and how they view and handle money. Emma will need to have patience with him, teach him *why* they need to budget and save money, and start working on the issue of money together.

Someone who is raised in the wealthy class may have a totally different outlook. Dr. Payne suggests that the wealthy class puts a high priority on investing and appearances, and those are just a few of the hidden rules within their class. If you were brought up in the middle class and married someone from the wealthy class, you may be frustrated that he does not want to spend anything and wants to invest money not only in stocks, but in your children's education. People in the wealthy class put a lot more emphasis on appearance than any other class, and think very differently about money in general.

In his book *Rich Dad, Poor Dad*, Robert Kiyosaki states that the rich think of money in a different way than the average middle class. Instead of thinking, "Can I afford this?" the rich think to themselves, "How can I afford this?" Opportunity is their best friend, and they are always searching for new ones.

In all of these scenarios, there are major communication issues. Communication in marriage is crucial, so you need to learn how to get on the same page financially. One way to do so is to realign your values as a couple. I created a worksheet for Mark and me, which I now call the Financial Bucket List (find it in Appendix A). This list helps you figure out what you want to do with your money and opens up the lines of communication between partners. The list is about seeing what your partner prioritizes in his or her life.

You first want to get together, print out two lists, and start by filling out your own list. *Then*, once you have filled out your list, you can come together and talk. Because you've done it separately you can be totally honest about your answers. This completed list will provide you with some talking points to help decide where you want to spend your money. It will show you the value systems you each have, and help you see where the other person is coming from.

When I first sat down and had this conversation with Mark, thoughts about where and how I was spending my money had never occurred to me. I know that sounds nonsensical, but I had never taken the time to sit and think to myself, "Where do I want my money to take me?" When we made our lists and then sat down and discussed them together, I realized many things. I wanted my kids to go to college without any student loan debt, and I wanted us to be able to retire comfortably and travel when we are older. I want a boat when my kids are older, so that we can go out on the water and have family days together. I was able to realize that my frivolous spending on things that really didn't matter in the long run was keeping me from achieving my long-term goals.

What changed me from being a careless Spender who would easily put $1,000 on a credit card for clothing without consulting my husband? The answer is, I made time to sit down and think about it. It's that simple—I forced myself to think about what I was doing.

If you are a Spender, I want you to ask yourself the following question this month and think about the answer in detail.

Where do you want your money to take you in life?

Find some time to grab a cup of tea or coffee and a quiet space, and reflect on your answer. Then start thinking about what you need to do to make some changes in your life to get there.

We should live life in the most meaningful way. You may have thought that you would want to pass your money on to your children or other family members. We want the ones we love to be taken care of, right?

You see, deeply held beliefs about money are manifested in individuals' financial behavior. You spend your money where your values lie. Sometimes we get our values mixed up because we lose track of life, things get too busy, or we never sit down to define those values in the first place.

Where do your values lie? Thinking about this shows you where your values are. It shows you what you care about. My guess is that you weren't thinking about upgrading your cable package or buying that new Coach purse you've been coveting. In fact, that question probably helped you to think about your money in a whole new light. You probably thought about your family, your faith, your job, or your health. Those things that you think about, those are your true values, so start making your spending a reflection of your true value system.

The great news is that you have today to make a good financial decision, and hopefully you have tomorrow and many more years to stick with those decisions. The lesson here? Take action *today* to start spending your money in a way that better reflects your values.

Don't let money issues add to the stress of your marriage. Start dealing with the underlying financial issues in your relationship, be aware of your cultural differences, make a Financial Bucket List together, and make your marriage flourish. It will take patience, time, and a lot of work, but the results can be beautiful!

Mark and I got into a good rhythm after a year. We would sit down on the last Sunday of every month to talk about the next month and set our budget. Mark would ask me questions like, "How much do you think you need for gifts this week?" and "Do you think you could work $150 in groceries this month, because we have an extra payment coming up?"

We would go through the budget line by line together. Sometimes we would disagree, but there was mutual respect. Mark would take the cash out every week and we would divide it into our budget envelopes.

We were on the same page, we both knew how much money we had to spend, and if one of us overspent we came back and talked to the other one. We became a well-oiled money couple, and people started to watch and comment about it. Suddenly younger couples started asking us how we talked about money, and we started having them over for dinner and teaching them.

The biggest reason we were able to be on the same page was because we were communicating *and* taking responsibility for our own actions. There was no more finger-pointing and blaming, only a team effort working toward the same goals.

In the years since we met with the first young couple over dinner, we've met with dozens of others. In every single case, it boils down to communication. Each and every couple we've met with was lacking appropriate communication with their spouse. There is lack of trust, anger, and resentment, and most were just flat-out ignoring it and had no idea how much debt they had.

Dealing with marriage and money is a lot like an airplane. As the airplane takes off, it can be a little bumpy at first, but you tell yourself it will be okay. When you hit that first layer of clouds and the plane begins to shake, you clutch the armrests and start getting nervous or afraid. Similarly in a marriage, as money troubles start to cloud the horizon, your marriage may start to feel a little shaky and you grab on to what comforts you. But like an ascending airplane, once you get past that first cloud cover you are in the open air and the flight is much smoother. The sun is shining, the air is clear, and there is beauty all around you. That doesn't mean that you won't hit an air pocket or some turbulence once in a while, but it does mean that you've weathered the storm together.

When it comes to your marriage and your money, don't quit at the first sight of clouds. Keep holding on and start talking about your money. If you work at it, you won't stay in the windy air and the bumpy clouds for the rest of your life, so hang on and get through the hard stuff. We went through it, and I can tell you from personal experience, *it is worth it*!

Chapter 8

From Spending Addict to Money Expert

The realization of how bad I was with money was a hard one to swallow. I was humiliated by my actions and embarrassed that I had gotten us into such a mess. Once I came to grips with my spending problem and why I wanted to stop, it was much easier for me to move forward. But even though things were starting to work, I was still afraid of falling off the wagon.

After we had that long talk one evening about the debt I had racked up, I knew we needed another income. I had a friend who was the manager at a local Ruth's Chris Steak House. I talked to him that night, and since I had previous restaurant experience, I got a job as a server there. For the next year and a half I worked five or six nights per week from around 3 p.m. until midnight. I would come home to a dark house, slip into bed, and then wake up at 6 a.m. to take care of my son while Mark rushed off to work. I made great money, which helped us start to pay off some of our debts. Having the extra income didn't help solve the spending problem I had, though. I would still find ways to spend extra cash. We would spend money on larger items, like a $4,000 fence for our backyard, or a swing set for our son. We were still in loads of debt, but we were making some progress. Despite the progress, I was having a really hard time and missed seeing my son every night. I wasn't able to put him to bed for almost a year and a half, and that made me so sad! I missed knowing what he liked to eat for dinner, and what his favorite bedtime story was. As much as I knew that this sacrifice was only for the short term, it was painful for me to say goodbye to him every day knowing how much he would miss me.

After I had worked a year and a half at the restaurant, Mark and I had paid down enough debt to have a different kind of conversation. We talked about my quitting my job to stay home with Andrew. I was exhausted working late nights in a stressful restaurant environment and just wanted to be home with my family. There were only three of us at that time, and we wanted to live a different kind of lifestyle. Mark and I worked opposite shifts and we missed each other. He worked from 8:00 a.m. to 4:30 p.m., and I worked from 3:00 p.m. to midnight. We had my sister-in-law watch Andrew from 2:30 to 4:30 every afternoon, and it was getting to be a hassle. We were always working. We took a look at our budget again and realized we were spending more than $1,000 per month on food. We ate out a lot, and spent a lot on groceries that would eventually spoil in our refrigerator from going uneaten. We figured that if I could cut our grocery bill down to only $200 per month and not go out to eat, we could afford for me to quit my job. We would still have debt payments to make, but we could continue to pay them off little by little, and I could be at home with my son. It seemed like that was a better choice for our family.

This is where our story begins to take another turn, because I was now presented with a new challenge—to cut our grocery bill from $1,000 to $200 per month. That meant we only had $50 per week to eat, and I had to make it work or else I was back to waiting tables. I Googled how to use coupons one night and a whole new world opened up to me. It was a game that I desperately wanted to master, so I set out to learn a new skill.

I learned how to coupon like a pro, mastering how to match coupons with sale items at Target, shop for larger items at BJ's to save money, and work the rebate programs at drugstores like Rite Aid, Walgreens, and CVS. I successfully fed our family on $50 per week for two years. I learned how to get toiletries, diapers, and food for almost free every single week. I was so excited about this that I taught my friends Colleen and Lindsay how to do it too, and we would frequently wake up at 5 a.m. to go to a triple coupon sale before our husbands went to work. We would shop together with hundreds of coupons in hand, looking to get hundreds of dollars of food for under $50. It was becoming my new addiction of a sort, but it was something that I felt good about. I was saving money, so that the money we had could go toward paying down the debt that I had incurred. It was my way to give back and contribute financially to my family.

I started posting pictures of my amazing grocery shopping trips on Facebook and on a tiny Blogspot blog I started. My friends were so amazed at my shopping trips, where I would carefully plan out how to get $400 in groceries for only $45, that they started asking me how I was doing it. I would have friends over in the evenings, and over coffee we would chat about how to use coupons. I would take friends out shopping at the grocery store and show them the ropes. I remember one night taking a young dating couple to the grocery store, showing them what they could buy for free and watching their faces light up at the checkout counter when they saw how much more they could get for their money.

I loved having this new expertise that others wanted to learn. The local moms' group I was a part of asked me if I could teach a coupon class for the group one night, and of course I said yes!

My first coupon class was for ten women in my moms' group. We sat in my living room and I shared my tips and tricks with them, showed them my massive three-inch coupon binder, which contained hundreds of coupons in baseball card organizers. Soon many of them started having success and were able to financially contribute to their families as well.

I taught about a half dozen free coupon classes throughout the year, mostly to church groups and friends and family. I loved sharing my secrets, but most of all it really helped me feel I was helping others. We were able to pay down a bit of debt that year because of the huge savings we had freed up in our budget, and suddenly I started seeing a light at the end of the tunnel. I was changing in so many ways. That giant mountain of debt I could never see over started shrinking and I could see the sun climbing over the top of the mountain. I was able to stick to a budget for the first time in my life, and I was actually enjoying it!

During this year, I also got pregnant with my second child. I was so sick during this pregnancy that I didn't coupon for most of the time. Thankfully I was still able to keep our grocery budget to around $75 per week because of the massive stockpile I had collected the year before. I had stocked up on so much free pasta, peanut butter, shampoo, conditioner, and razors that we practically didn't have to buy toiletries for the entire year. We ended up eating out a lot because I was so tired and sick during the pregnancy, so we stopped making extra debt payments, but we were careful to not incur any more debt. I was a changed woman. I wasn't spending money, I had stopped impulsively buying, and I respected the boundaries that we had put in place with our budget.

Right after the birth of my second child, we received word that Mark's job was in jeopardy. His company had merged with another one and they were going to be doing layoffs. He was the last one who was hired, so he was the first on the chopping block. I remember exactly where we were sitting when we got the call. We had just finished registering our son for pre-K and we were walking around our favorite pond in the woods near our neighborhood. We had our five-day-old baby nestled in a baby carrier on my chest, and our four-year-old running around like boys do. Mark received the call, and our world crashed around us. During the next six weeks we would learn that we would have to move back to New York from South Carolina, where we were living. Mark got offered his old job back in New York, so we moved back home into his parents' basement. We had been on our way to a debt-free life, and in a moment all of our plans, our hard work, our successes came falling down around us.

Six weeks later we moved back to our home state of New York. We sold as a short sale the 3,200-square-foot home that was killing us. We were able to get approved for a short sale due to Mark's job insecurity, and because ten homes on our street were about to go into foreclosure. When we sold our house for $190,000 to a cash buyer, it was a true miracle! The stress of selling a huge house while having a newborn baby proved to be taxing but not impossible. We were finally going to be free from the stress of that huge mortgage payment and well on our way to paying down more debt.

We had to go into $4,000 more debt to move; we didn't have any other option. Mark's parents let us borrow this sum with terms that we would pay it back as soon as possible and with interest. Three years to the day after moving to South Carolina, we drove back to New York with all of our belongings in a moving truck behind us, just like we had three years earlier. We had one more child and less debt, and were free from many of the terrible financial mistakes we had made over those past three years. I felt as if we had been given a second chance at life.

When we first moved back to New York, we were homeless. We lived with Mark's parents for a week, and then moved into my sister's house for a few weeks. She was pregnant with her first child, and we only had about three or four weeks to stay with her until she was due with her baby.

We debated owning versus renting a house, but because we had just done a short sale on our property, we couldn't qualify for another mortgage right away. We opted to rent, and went searching for something that was large enough for our family of four.

We found a rental town house and nestled into the 800-square-foot home. We sold most of what we owned for cash to help pay down debt, except for a few beds and a single couch. The house was so small that we didn't have room for our kitchen supplies, so we kept them in shelves out in the garage. Despite the tight quarters, we were happy. We were finally free of the big house that had been a struggle to afford and were back near our family again. I missed my old friends in South Carolina terribly, but I knew this was the best decision for our family.

In the months after we moved back, I learned that couponing was not as easy in New York as it had been in South Carolina. I had to learn all new store policies, and with the lack of a local blogger providing all of the sale matchups, I was feeling the stress of an increasing grocery budget. But within five months I was back down to my $50-per-week budget and getting my friends to play along too. I started to post more and more pictures on Facebook of how I got free stuff using coupons. My friends wanted to know more!

With so many people wanting me to teach them, I decided to start a coupon class. I had done at least twelve of them back in South Carolina, teaching hundreds of people how to cut their grocery bills successfully, so I felt it was the right time to start charging for the class. I thought that maybe if I charged, I could make a little extra cash for my time and earn back my investment for the packets I printed out for the class. I also knew that if people pay for something they are more likely to show up—I was sick of people standing me up for classes when I had already paid to have the printouts made for them.

My first coupon class in New York had thirty people in attendance. I charged $10 per person and made $300 cash that night. I was thrilled, but I didn't know what to do with the money. I wondered if we should pay down more debt, or if I should invest it back into my coupon class in some way. Everyone at the class kept asking if I would start a website to help them on a weekly basis, but I wasn't sure if that was what I wanted to do.

After reading a few blogs online, I knew that somehow people were making money by blogging, even though I had no idea how. At that time, we really needed the extra income since we wanted to send our son to preschool that year. In May 2010, as I stood at my kitchen sink washing dinner dishes, I asked myself, "What would I call a website? I mean, I am just *that* lady you get stuck behind in the grocery store, right?"

There it was! Like a lightbulb turning on over my head, I repeated to myself, "I am THAT Lady." That was what I would call my website! I rushed over to my computer and searched to see if the domain name was taken, and it wasn't! I was thrilled, and that night I purchased the website name *I am THAT Lady*, which is now laurengreutman.com. I had no idea what this would mean, but I knew that it was another way for me to help others, and maybe earn a little extra money on the side to help pay for my son's preschool while continuing to pay down our debt.

I continued to teach coupon classes and had graduated to hosting them at local newspaper offices per their request. Suddenly I started receiving requests to appear on our local news stations. It was such a thrill as I started to get more and more readers visiting my website. What excited me the most was that so many of these people were women facing similar struggles to mine about getting out of debt, paying their bills, and having enough to feed their family healthy food.

I put in forty hours per week on my little website that I had my brother-in-law design using the $300 from that first coupon class. I still had no idea how to make money blogging, but I worked hard to create something that I knew would help other women save on their groceries. An entire year had passed and I had finally learned how to make money doing what I loved and was good at. At first I was earning around $200 each month on the blog, getting paid from companies to get people to print coupons from my website, as well as money I made from private advertising. It equaled about $1.25 per hour considering the amount of time I was putting into it each week. Some may say it was a waste of time (and I had friends and family who did), but that $200 per month was *huge* for us! That meant that we could afford to send our son to the private Christian preschool we wanted him to attend, and have some extra cash to pay down more debt.

I was also pregnant with our third child, and knew that our expenses would increase with the welcome addition. We started planning ahead. During my pregnancy I learned how to bring in even more money. I started taking home surveys and using Swagbucks to earn extra cash, participating in market research, selling things on eBay, and learning how to increase my earnings through the blog. With the appearances on my local news stations, more people started to visit the blog, which meant I was getting paid more from advertisers. I also started to learn how to do affiliate marketing and started earning a percentage of every purchase someone would make through one of my links. For example, if there was a sale on toilet paper on Amazon, I would post the deal on my website with an affiliate link (provided to me by Amazon) and earn a small percentage of the sale. Those small percentages add up when multiple people purchase, so I started to learn how to do more and more affiliate posts. When my third child was born, everything started to change with the website. The reality television show *Extreme Couponing* had become popular on TLC.

All of a sudden young people were starting to come out in droves to my coupon seminars. They wanted to learn more, so they would read my blog and share it with their friends. My website income started to grow and we were able to pay off more and more debt. It was such an exciting time, because I finally felt I was making a substantial contribution to our family finances.

I continued to write for *I am THAT Lady* (now laurengreutman .com) and teach live coupon seminars for the next few years. As a spending addict now in recovery, I was so excited to share with everyone what I had learned through the process. I knew the exact changes I had made that really made a difference, and I was having a lot of success using my life experiences to teach others how to do the same thing. I had come full circle and now found pleasure in helping others get through the rough terrain that I had been through a few years before.

Mark got a raise at work that year as well, accelerating our debt repayment even more. We found out we were pregnant with baby number four, and our credit cards started to disappear one at a time, until we finally paid them all off. Finally, after all our hard work, we wrote the last check to our student loan company in February 2012. This was the final debt repayment. It was official! We had paid off more than $40,000 worth of car payments, credit card bills, and student loans in just under four years!

It was not an easy journey, but here I am six years after starting that website writing this book for you. I've been through a lot, from a chronic spending addiction to recovery to teaching, and am now valued as an expert who has literally helped millions of women along the way. I've been featured on shows like *The Dr. Oz Show*, *Good Morning America*, *Fox & Friends*, and the *Today* show. They keep asking me to come back on their shows, because my story resonates with so many and this is an issue that affects millions.

A 2015 study by NerdWallet reported that the average American household credit card debt is more than $15,000, with national consumer debt at $712 *billion*! Those are *huge* numbers, and I know firsthand what it's like to be one of those consumers drowning in debt. I've been there, I know what to do, and I know how to get out. It's not just about increasing your income or decreasing your bills, even though those are all things I teach. It's really about the vision, emotions, and values behind what you are doing with your money.

In the past few years, I've had the pleasure of sitting down with and helping many people who need help with their finances. I've realized that people can do anything they put their minds to if they want it bad enough. I wanted to get out of debt and change my life so badly that I literally changed everything—from my mind-set, to where I lived, to how I spent and viewed money. I want that for you, too. You may not become a nationally known money expert like me, but you can become a money expert for yourself and your family.

Chapter 9

Getting Emotional About Your Spending

My dear grandma Roberts always told me there are three things you should never discuss in public: sex, politics, and money. We can all agree that our society has given up on secrecy about the first two, but somehow the topic of money is still taboo. You may feel as if you are the only one who struggles with spending, but the reality is that many people do, it's just that no one talks about it.

We've all known about "keeping up with the Joneses." The writer and personality Quentin Crisp said, "Never keep up with the Joneses. Drag them down to your level. It's cheaper." I wonder how many of those Joneses, if truth be told, are as rich as you think they are. If you've been trying to keep up with them, you may have been trying to keep up with a lie the whole time. And that lie is responsible for making you dead broke and stressed out.

Think about how you spend right now. What choices are you making? Are those choices for now, or are they for tomorrow? Do you continue to make purchases with a credit card despite being in credit card debt? What will the ultimate consequences of your spending be? What changes do you need to make now?

These are all questions that I asked myself during my darkest hours. I had to analyze the consequences of continuing my bad spending habits, in my case those included losing my home, continuing to live a life full of debt, possibly raising children who have no concept of money, and—even worse—losing my marriage. Suddenly, the difficulties of changing my spending habits appeared much easier to face than the consequences of staying the same. I had to make a choice, and that meant drastic changes. It meant learning about myself, what my triggers were, and getting *emotional* about my money. How in the world had I charged $12,000 in one night to earn a free car and *not* get upset about it? How had that happened? I wanted to know why, so I started digging into my motivations to learn how to stop myself from this compulsive behavior.

I realized that the main causes of my overspending were impulsive purchases, boredom, the confusion between wants versus needs, and an inability to say no to myself. This was evident in my life in many different ways.

I wanted to learn how to play the guitar my junior year of college, so I bought a $600 guitar without doing any research. I remember telling Mark at the time, and he was shocked that I had bought it without sleeping on the decision or doing any comparative shopping. The thought of doing those two things never even crossed my mind; it was a totally impulsive decision.

The same lack of self-control kicked in when I would buy my son a new Lightning McQueen toy every time we went to Target (which was about two or three times per week—another issue of self-control). I wanted him to be happy, and it was only a few dollars, I would tell myself.

What I didn't realize was that I was teaching him that he could get whatever he wanted, whenever he wanted it, something that I was struggling to unlearn.

I realized I was not the only person with spending issues, so I set out to research and hear from other women with the same issues. In the survey I sent out to my e-mail list, more than 2,200 women answered. The women were between the ages of twenty and eighty-three, with the majority of respondents from twenty-five to forty. I wanted to see if there were common traits and emotional characteristics shared by Spenders. I also wanted to see why these women thought they overspent and if they too felt out of control.

I asked the women these eight questions:

1. Do you currently overspend and go over budget?
2. Why do you think you overspend?
3. What do you think would help you learn how to stop overspending?
4. Do you feel out of control with your spending?
5. What is your age?
6. How do you feel before you spend money?
7. How do you feel while you are spending money?
8. What do you feel after you've spent money?

THE SURVEY RESULTS

Seventy-three percent of my respondents admitted to being overspenders. That is a *huge* majority, and a number that should help you realize that you are not alone! Thousands of others are dealing with this same issue. There is hope for them, and so there is hope for you too!

Here are some of the responses from the survey results when asked why they think they overspend:

- If I overspend, it's because of discretionary spending and typical impulse buys.
- I generally go shopping without a list, then end up buying way too many unnecessary things!
- Lack of planning, impulse buys
- After a long time going without, we now have wiggle room again and we use it.
- I am trying to keep everyone happy, even when we can't afford it.
- I don't think about the impact while in the moment.
- Lack of planning and peer pressure
- Lack of planning/stress shopping
- Because I always say this one is an "exception"—next month I'll do better.
- See something on sale and can't pass it up
- Having trouble with needs versus wants, not having time to budget
- Sometimes necessity, other times to give my daughter the best life possible, to nurture relationships
- Try to get on a budget, but husband won't fully commit
- I get depressed about having no money so I end up spending even more money, then feel terrible about it later!

My research shows that the number one thing Spenders think will help them is learning how to stick to a budget successfully. If they are the one who is trying to budget, oftentimes they blame their spouse for why they fail.

As happy as I am knowing that I am not alone in my spending woes, I am saddened to think that so many women are like me. Even though I am currently in recovery, I know that one mistake can put me right back in the same boat as so many others. What I found in the survey is that of the 73 percent who said they overspend, 48 percent admitted to feeling happy before they spend money, increasing to 59 percent feeling happy during a spending spree, then plummeting to a low of 43 percent citing feelings of happiness after they spend money.

Some of the replies I saw in the survey made me realize why happiness is such a common feeling among Spenders. Here are actual responses from people who report that they are happier when spending money:

- My feelings vary greatly. Sometimes neutral, sometimes very gratified, other times wish I would have shown better restraint.
- Emotional. I'm depressed. Shopping makes me happy.
- I am constantly seeking perfection and happiness.
- I overspend when I get excited or want to try something new.
- Need for immediate gratification
- To feel better from stress of life
- To make my kids happy
- It makes me feel better.

This suggests that there is something happening in the brain of Spenders that may be boosting their endorphin levels during the spending process.

A shocking 56 percent of women who admitted they are Spenders also admitted to feeling guilty after they spend money. The majority of that 56 percent reported that they felt their overspending was a result of a lack of planning and impulse purchases. Here are some of the common responses of women who felt guilty after they overspent:

- I want things I can't have.
- I am bipolar and am an emotional spender.
- I don't know how to budget properly.
- I spend because I want things that I can't have.
- I get bored and shop for fun.
- I spend more when I am depressed.
- I tell myself I will pay it off, but that never happens.
- I am tempted to spend money and do not plan around that.
- I want to make my family happy, so I spend money on them.
- I am very impulsive.
- I go out to eat too much because of lack of planning.
- It's not my fault; my husband buys things he doesn't need.
- There are too many deals to pass up.

Since I am representative of the women in this group (even though my opinions were not included in the survey), I can relate to all of the answers. You spend money when you don't have a plan, then you make impulsive purchases and have no idea where your money goes. You try to stick to a budget, but don't really know how to set one up so that it actually works. Because you don't budget, you fail at handling your finances. This vicious cycle continues over and over again.

IS DEPRESSION THE TRIGGER OR A RESULT?

What I found interesting in my research is that 21 percent of overspenders say they feel depressed before spending, but that goes down to only 10 percent who feel depressed as they are spending money. After they spend money, however, the depressed feeling shoots back up to 17 percent. The bottom line? There are a lot of women who are spending money when they are depressed, and even though they may feel slightly less depressed while spending, they are likely to spiral back down into feelings of depression and guilt afterward.

In between graduating college and my stint in the home-based business, I worked as a drug and alcohol counselor at an outpatient treatment center. I graduated college with a degree in criminal justice, and took a lot of courses on how addiction and drugs affect brain chemistry. I got an internship at a drug treatment court right out of college, fell in love with the counseling world, and got my first professional job.

While I was working at the outpatient clinic, I conducted independent counseling as well as group sessions. When evaluating our incoming clients, it was often hard to figure out if the addiction or the mental illness came first.

Growing up, I saw mental illness and addiction firsthand. My older brother, Rick, was first diagnosed with ADHD as a young boy, which later became a bipolar diagnosis. Rick began experimenting with drugs at a very young age, and by the age of sixteen he was using hard drugs like cocaine and heroin. He was an addict for ten years, often living on the streets of New York City or in friends' cars. We were all devastated when his life spiraled into full-blown addiction. We missed the brother that we had grown up with, and desperately wanted him to be well again.

We would occasionally hear from him and know that he was alive, but that he had been seduced by his dream of living a life without responsibilities. He would often change his mind about his lifestyle and get himself into rehab. His desire to change would disappear once he was out of rehab, though, and back in his old environment. He would start using almost immediately because the temptation was just too strong and he didn't have strong enough boundaries in place to stay clean.

At the age of twenty-six, my brother hanged himself while in a prison cell. He was a kind and loving brother, but eventually the addiction and mental illness got the best of him. After he died, I had such guilt. I had smoked with him dozens of times—he introduced me to it, actually. I ran in a bad crowd with him for years. It had never become anything more than a casual thing for me. Addiction is something that runs in my family, and even though my addiction was not heroin like my brother's was, my drug of choice had become shopping.

I always wanted to find out why I overspent; it was always an emotional thing for me. I would feel depressed or bored, then spend money, and feel better for a while, then would feel depressed again. Eventually, a few days later, the cycle would repeat itself.

It wasn't until I was able to learn how to budget, use cash, and track my spending that I was able to make rational decisions with my money. What I found is that when I tracked my spending, it took away the emotional and addictive part of shopping for me. It helped me stay away from those spur-of-the moment purchases and become less stressed, less depressed, and more focused.

Chapter 10

Triggers and Your Money Personality

A trigger is defined by Dictionary.com as anything, an act or event, that serves as a stimulus and initiates or precipitates a reaction or series of reactions. Many overspenders documented in my survey identified their triggers as:

- Fear
- Good deals they cannot pass up
- Boredom
- Anxiety
- Depression
- Lack of planning
- Hungry when shopping for food
- Excitement
- Happiness
- Not a care in the world
- Ignorance

- Stress
- Overwhelmed with life—escape

In order to stop spending money, you have to learn your triggers and how to stop them before they cause you to spend.

The majority of the women who reported their triggers also stated that they need help sticking to a budget from someone who has been through it before, and that they would like more help from a spouse to keep things on track.

Spenders like spending money, but they often do not feel great about it afterward. If you as a Spender can identify the triggers that lead to guilt, you can stop the guilt from happening before it starts.

I know this from personal experience. After I charged the $12,000 on a credit card in a single night and won that free car, I didn't feel that bad. But over time, the guilt and shame of it started to creep up on me. I stopped recruiting people into my unit, because I stopped believing in the lies of the company.

I saw many other stay-at-home moms who wanted to make a little extra cash by doing a home-based business, but what they didn't see was that they were the first customer to the company. As long as they bought product, the company didn't care how much they sold or how much money they made. Such companies (and many other home-based business models) prey on the stay-at-home mom to make extra cash, then load them up with products and debt and promise them a better future for their families.

I started to become jaded in this business model and angry at the company that I had gone into severe debt over. I eventually walked away from them, gave back my "free" car, and apologized to many of my unit members, who were also drowning in debt.

So why does the pattern continue to happen to some? Maybe because the Spender does not identify themselves as having a problem? Maybe you are not sure if you would be considered a Spender in need of recovery?

To help you to diagnose your spending personality, here are the seven types of behaviors common to compulsive shoppers. These seven behaviors were identified by the Shulman Center for Compulsive Theft, Spending, and Hoarding.

1. Are you an emotional shopper?

You are an emotional shopper if you shop to distract yourself from how you are feeling. You often shop when you are depressed or anxious to help alleviate some of the uncomfortable feelings.

2. Are you a trophy shopper?

Trophy shoppers often shop because they need just one more item to complete an outfit. They typically look for high-dollar items.

3. Are you an image shopper?

If you are an image shopper, you shop to look good. You often pick up the tab at the bar, drive a nice car, and wear expensive clothing. That is because you have to look like you have a lot of money.

4. Are you a bargain shopper?

Bargain shoppers get into trouble because they can't pass up a good deal. Extreme couponers and hoarders would fall into this category, as well as people who love to shop for deals.

5. Are you a codependent shopper?

You shop to gain approval. If you are out for a night with your girl-friends and they want to stop and shop, you buy because they buy.

6. Are you a "bulimic" shopper?

If you buy things, then return them, then buy and return another item, you may be what is considered a "bulimic" shopper.

7. Are you a collector shopper?

Do you buy things to complete a collection? The thrill of having a complete collection, or various dresses in the same color because you love them, would put you into the collector shopping category.

If you fit into one of these seven categories, you have a shopping problem. If you never admit to yourself that you have a problem, you will never be able to break the cycle of spending.

I fall into many of these categories, and although I am now in recovery, I still find myself thinking about sales at thrift stores. I fit into three categories at different points of my life. While I was in the home-based business I was a trophy shopper. Before that I was an emotional shopper, and afterward I became a bargain shopper.

To make it worse, I was completely uneducated about my finances. I had no idea what compound interest was or how to save money. I hadn't thought about how my spending reflected my values, and I was just too passive to look at the other side of the credit card bill where the interest rates were explained. I wasn't taught anything about money in school, and felt totally unprepared to handle it in the real world.

I had to learn what my triggers are so that I could avoid them. Here is a list of some of my triggers and the boundaries I've set up for myself over the years.

- I do not go to home-based product parties—Thirty-One, Tupperware, Pampered Chef, or any others. I say no, because I know I will buy something that I don't need and/or wouldn't be able to afford. I also do not support their business model, so I prefer not to go to their parties.
- I do not go shopping at the mall alone.
- I only use cash, and do not use credit cards for personal expenses. I do have one credit card for business transactions so I can earn airline miles to fly.
- I shop for my kids at thrift stores and online consignment websites. I have no self-control when it comes to little sparkly girls' clothing. I have three young daughters and cannot control myself.
- I do not buy anything from someone who is having a fund-raiser or selling cookies. If you come to my front door and ask me for money, I will say no 100 percent of the time. Not because I don't care, but because it is one of the triggers for me to overspend.
- I do not do expensive or elaborate birthday parties for my kids.
- I do not go into home decorating stores, because I would feel that my home was not pretty enough. I tend to be more minimalist because I can often feel "less than."

Learning my triggers and getting emotional about where my money was going was a huge part of my recovery process, but it wasn't an overnight success. Getting the hang of this for yourself will take a few months, but it is much easier to say no before you are triggered than when you are stuck right in the middle of an emotion.

Once you have your triggers identified and your boundaries set, you are on your way. Just yesterday I was asked on Facebook to attend a book party. My exact words to the person inviting me were, "I don't attend at-home parties. It is one of my triggers, and in order to stay out of debt and not overspend, I say no to every one I am invited to."

Anytime you get asked to one, feel free to use my response, subbing out the appropriate words. It is freeing to already have a response prepared, and the person asking should now understand why you had to say no.

THE BRAIN OF A SPENDER

As I dug deeper to understand my emotions and spending triggers, I pulled out an old college textbook about drugs and the brain. Because of watching my brother's life, I was inspired to help others like him who struggled with addictions in their lives. The funny thing is that after learning about addiction and what happens in the brain, I realized I wasn't much different from my brother. I just had a different drug of choice.

In my research I learned what happens inside the brain of a Spender. I wanted to know—is spending addiction a real thing? In order to stop spending money, I thought it was crucial to truly understand what was happening in my mind when I spent. By knowing this, I hoped I could then halt the process before it began.

When you think about it, a purchase is simply an exchange that involves a trade-off for the pleasure of spending that money against the pain of losing the potential of whatever else the money could do. I'll use the example from chapter 1 of my winning a car. When I put all that money on my credit card, I was saying that I valued what the car provided me more than I valued the money. I valued the prize of the car more than the idea of living debt-free. I found that surprising, because I had always thought my value system included providing for my family and taking good care of them. Spending $12,000 in one night on a credit card went against my core values, but at that moment I didn't think about it as a trade-off.

In a "Spendthrift-Tightwad" study conducted by Scott I. Rick and colleagues, in the *Journal of Consumer Research*, researchers studied what happens in the brains of people with poor spending habits. They gave $40 to each subject, then used an MRI to record brain activity as subjects were shown pictures of various consumer items. Researchers saw that whenever one of the people they were studying liked an item they saw in a photo, the place in the brain responsible for pleasure, the nucleus accumbens, lit up. Have you ever touched a sweater in a store, said to yourself, "I love this," then bought it immediately? Did you pause to think about how much money it cost or how you were going to pay for it? If not, then your nucleus accumbens took over and sent a signal to your brain that pretty much said, "Buy this now!"

The insula is the part of the brain that does the opposite of what the nuclear accumbens does. It is responsible for many things, including reading the psychological state of the entire body and generating feelings that can motivate actions. For instance, if you are about to slam your hand in your car door, the insula will alert your body and tell it to take action and pull the hand away. If you are hungry, it will tell the body to take action and eat. If you are broke and at a mall, it will tell you to take action and get out before you get yourself into trouble. The researchers found that when subjects were shown the prices of the items, the insula reacted and the person decided not to purchase the item. When the insula did not light up, the person got all of the pleasure from the nucleus accumbens and ultimately decided to spend their money.

The more stimulation inside the insula, the less likely you are to keep spending money. In other words, when it comes to money, increased insula stimulation can stop your spending.

So what does all this mean? Can we change the way our brain alerts us when we are overspending? The point of this knowledge isn't just to say, "It's my brain's fault!" Instead, we can now make educated decisions about how to protect ourselves from overspending.

As a Spender struggling to get your spending in check, you have to get to the point where the pain of not spending money is less than that of dealing with the consequences of your overspending. As someone who used to have the hardest time resisting a new pair of shoes the second I saw them, this was a major challenge for me. I had gotten to the point where the stress and weight of the debt I was under was paralyzing, and I was finally ready to make a change.

NEW YORK CITY AND THE *TODAY* SHOW

Recently I was in New York to record a segment with Kathie Lee and Hoda on the *Today* show. I've wanted to be on *Today* ever since I was a little girl. I watched the Macy's Thanksgiving Day Parade every year and always thought it would be so glamorous to go on the show. Tomorrow would be the big day! I would be talking about how to make your next year $10,000 richer, using the tips and strategies that I had used to get out of debt. I consider it such a blessing to be able to teach thousands of people what I know. And I love the hustle and bustle of New York City for a day or two. After that, I'm ready to return to my humble home upstate with my family.

The first place I headed was Times Square. I really enjoy seeing what the new and upcoming entertainment events are, and all that is happening in the craziness that is Times Square. Did you know they have an entire store in the middle of the square devoted to Hello Kitty? Yes—an *entire* Hello Kitty store! My daughters would be in heaven!

In front of me was the famous Jumbotron filled with advertisements. I counted more than fifty TV screens all over the sides of the tall Manhattan buildings. In the background I heard people selling a tour bus ride or a ticket to the latest show, all over the sound of sirens, car horns, and the steady buzz of the crowds.

In the center of Times Square there are benches set up like bleachers at a high school football game facing the Jumbotron, and they are always filled with people stopping for a moment to take it all in. Around the bleacher-type seats are tables and chairs. All of the tables are always filled with spectators taking videos and pictures of their surroundings. Times Square is one place where you really understand you are being sold to (at least I hope you do). Your senses are bombarded with the enormous lighted signs and videos, but if you know what's going on you can enjoy the experience instead of escaping through shopping.

As I scanned the crowds, I saw all sorts of people from all different walks of life. You can find police officers working hard to protect the city. There are people from every nationality imaginable, children and their parents, college students, professionals, the elderly, New Yorkers and tourists alike. I sat there wondering what was going on in everyone's life. I wanted to know what their lives were like financially, because everyone looked successful on the surface.

That's the way it is in life. You see so many people every day, try to keep up with what it looks like those people have, but do you ever stop to figure out what it really is that you are chasing? Are you chasing someone else's dream? Did your neighbor get a new Lexus, and now you think you should have one? As I stood in the middle of Times Square, I was overwhelmed with gratitude that I had stopped running the rat race of trying to keep up with the Joneses. There are so many Joneses, but only one path for me and my family.

Chapter 11

The Crisis Point

In a moment of crisis, a person's value system often shifts. Crises are hard to go through, but typically people come out better on the other side. When I came clean to Mark about our debt, I put myself in a crisis moment. Let me remind you that we were in a money crisis for a long time, but we never took any action to fix it. I could have continued to ignore it even longer, but I had had enough and knew that I had to stop. After our conversation in the bedroom that night, we decided to put ourselves into crisis mode so that we could change our lives forever.

I was so sick and tired of being broke all the time and pretending I had it all together. I felt there was more to life than just buying things on credit cards, struggling to pay the bills, and then repeating the process all over again. I knew that there is more to life than spending money, but why is it so hard to do?

If you are currently making enough money to live on, but are continuing to use credit cards, you may not yet be at that point of crisis that will force you to make changes. But what if you lose your job and suddenly find yourself in crisis mode? What will you do then?

I hear from people every day that they had a sudden job loss and were left with no savings and no backup plan. That is a crisis I don't want you to face. You don't have to wait until a crisis hits that is out of your control. Take a look at your finances *now*, **put yourself in crisis mode**, and figure out how to fix what isn't working. To avoid finding yourself in an uncontrollable situation caused by a terrible life event, plan ahead and create your own opportunity to figure out *why* you are spending and how to fix it.

How do you know if you are in a money crisis? If you answer yes to any of the questions below, you most likely are in a money crisis.

- Are you spending more money each month than you are making?
- Are you in debt but refuse to get rid of luxury items like your cable or iPhone?
- Are you in credit card debt and have no idea how you are going to pay it off?
- Do you have credit card debt and continue to use your credit card with no plan for paying it off?
- Do you have no idea how much money is in your bank account at this moment?
- Do you not know how to create a monthly budget?
- Do you refinance or take out payday loans to afford your monthly bills?
- Do you feel out of control with your money?
- Are you frequently missing credit card payments and incurring late fees?
- Are debt collectors calling your house?
- Do you frequently sign up for zero percent introductory-rate credit cards to transfer your higher-interest-rate bills?

- Do you pay for extra cable TV channels to watch football, but put your groceries on a credit card?
- Are you over the age of forty and have *zero* retirement savings?
- Does more than 20 percent of your monthly take-home pay go to loan payments?
- Do you have maxed-out credit cards?
- Does shopping cause distress in your relationships?
- Do you shop to deal with negative feelings?

If you answered yes to any one of these, you have a problem. If you answered yes to two or more, you are in a money crisis. You now have a choice to make: Do you want to continue to live this way, or are you ready to make a change?

Start now and change your spending to reflect your values while you still have control, before you are forced to change later on. Ben Franklin said, "Money never made a man happy yet, nor will it. The more a man has, the more he wants." Is your spending truly making you happy? Really, truly, deep down in your bones happy? My guess is no, because Spenders spend to fill a void, then once that high wears off they need to spend again. Spending like this will never make you happy, and a Chronic Spender will never spend in line with her values until she realizes this.

In order to make your spending a reflection of your values, you need to focus on creating a budget that reflects what you hold dear. If you really want your kids to go to college, then you should start saving and freeing up money in your monthly budget so you can make that a reality.

Ask yourself right now, what are you unwilling to give up at the expense of being in debt? Why is that? Are you so accustomed to living the way you want that you refuse to be uncomfortable for a brief time in your life? Do you refuse to give up some things because you don't know how you will function without them? Remember, the sacrifice isn't forever; it is temporary. But if you never start sacrificing your wants to your needs, this pattern just might follow you around for the rest of your life.

The things you are not willing to give up and change are the things keeping you from a true value switch. That mind-set and those things are holding you back from a stress-free and debt-free life.

As I went through this process myself, I realized there was a lot that I was unwilling to give up. The list included eating at restaurants, the freedom to buy what I want when I want it, clothing, impulse purchases, toys for my kids, and much more! I wish I could tell you that once I realized this I quickly changed my priorities. I didn't. It was a long process to get to where I am, and it started with learning the B-word. Budget.

Budgets are something that every Spender runs from. The good news is that I found a few secrets for creating a successful budget for Spenders, and in the next chapter I'll share them with you.

Chapter 12

The Fences and Budgets

One of my favorite things to do in the morning before my kids wake up is to sit at the kitchen table, drink my coffee, and read my Bible. One particular morning at 6:00 a.m., I was staring out the window enjoying the view of the birds eating at my bird feeder. I remember thinking how beautiful they were, when there was a loud thump as something big and heavy hit the window. The window shook and I went outside to see what had happened. A beautiful red-bellied robin had flown directly into my window and died. As I picked it up and placed it in a shoe box, I thought about this bird. I wondered what had happened that had led up to its fatal accident with my kitchen window.

I imagined that the bird saw all of its friends at the feeder and thought, "Hey, look at them, they look like they've got something fun going on." And as he flew by he lost track of where he was going and flew into the window.

Was the bird wrong for wanting to see what everyone else was doing? No, he was just curious and wanted to feel a part of the group.

As Spenders we are like that bird. We like to spend because it's fun and necessary, just like flying is for a bird. Shopping is a fun activity to do with your kids or with your friends. You need to shop for groceries and toiletries, your kids need underwear, and you need laundry detergent. Spending is just as necessary to our life as flying is to a bird. If one bad habit develops about spending money, however, you may have a financial catastrophe coming your way. Just like the bird who didn't see the window in front of it, you won't see your financial crash until it's too late.

When I was spending money with abandon for years, there were times I would try to stop. Mark and I would make a budget together as we sat down and talked about saving for our future and paying off the enormous amount of debt we were in. But when I actually got out in the real world, I failed miserably. Just like the bird who lost control, I would lose control of myself by making just one financial mistake.

It didn't just start when I was married, though. Mark had married a person with a shopping addiction, but I don't think he knew how far gone I was.

Even though I was the second of four children, I had a typical first-born personality. I am an all-or-nothing person. I either do something all the way and am an overachiever and perfectionist, or I throw up my hands when things get too hard and give up.

The thrill of spending money caught me at an early age, but what I didn't see when I was growing up is that many of my behaviors were big red flags to an addiction. I am very impulsive, and I rarely learn from my mistakes. I get into things all the way and don't often foresee the consequences. I would spend money on things that I didn't need to fill a hole that I didn't know was there. I had a constant need for more clothing and things and felt better when I got them.

Looking back at that time in my life now as a Recovering Spender, I see that I was addicted to spending. As someone who loved to spend money frivolously, I really wrestled with the idea of setting a budget. It just seemed way too strict.

A BUDGET FOR A SPENDER CAN BE COMPARED TO INPATIENT TREATMENT FOR A DRUG ADDICT

A budget puts a Spender's money in a treatment program of some sort.

My husband, Mark, is an actuary, which means he loves numbers, calculations, and spreadsheets. When we first got married, he would call me over to the computer to show me an awesome formula he had come up with to calculate a mortality table he needed for work. I would commend him on a job well done and walk away overwhelmed and confused.

I would rather stick a pencil in my eye than look at a spreadsheet. They make me break out in a cold sweat. If you are a Spender, I bet you are giggling to yourself right now because you feel the exact same way.

Despite Mark's math major and spreadsheet skills, I was the one who took charge of our finances when we were first married. My mom was always the one who took care of our money when I was growing up, so I thought that was my job as a wife.

I remember walking in on her while she was paying the bills one day. She always wrote her budget in a large eight-by-ten leather-bound journal. She would sit in the dining room surrounded by bills, writing down all of the numbers and adding them up to make sure they were correct. There were many occasions where she would show me the numbers and how they were not adding up, then give me the proverbial "money doesn't grow on trees" speech that all parents are obligated to give at least once in their lifetime.

My parents paid for their first nice house in cash from the sale of another house that they had rehabbed when they were first married. They later built a larger house, which drastically changed their month-to-month budget. With four kids, ballet lessons, inpatient drug treatments for my brother, and my two sisters who liked to ski and do gymnastics, their budget had gotten very tight. There were many months where my mom would have only $50.00 for groceries, but she always found a way to make it work. She wasn't one to complain much, and did her best to provide a calm and welcoming home.

When we were married at twenty-one, I thought it was my responsibility to take care of our money because it was what my mom had done. It wasn't a conversation we ever had, it just happened. I took over and Mark didn't say anything. Ignore the fact that the year prior to our getting married, I was in $5,000 worth of credit card debt as a sophomore in college. Thankfully, I was rescued by my grandpa Roberts, who paid off the bills shortly before I left school that year. But once again I didn't have to take responsibility for my mistakes.

I should never have been the one to handle our money, but Mark didn't know any better because we had never really talked about money prior to getting married. Had he known my spending history, it might have been a different story.

I sat in our tiny two-bedroom apartment as a newlywed, with my new eight-by-ten leather-bound notebook, the exact same kind my mother had used, and started writing down what we were spending. I would take a look at our bank statement, make categories, and place our transactions under those categories. The first month we were married we spent $1,000 at Walmart! I should tell you that we were living off of our wedding-gift money, student loans, and Mark's $100-a-week tutoring job.

That was the first time I actually thought about budgeting. I didn't want to spend all of our income at Walmart, but I didn't really know how to go about starting to budget. As a Spender, a budget sounded like prison. I decided I wouldn't budget yet, but really just track how much we were spending, and if something got out of control we would stop spending money on that.

Years and years of uncontrolled spending was the result. I continued to be in charge of our finances, because that is what you are supposed to do as a wife (or so I thought). I would take out my eight-by-ten leather-bound notebook and write down where our money was going. And it continued to fly out of our hands faster than we could make it. As I wrote on the neat lined paper, I realized I had no idea what I was doing. I knew I wasn't good at keeping track of our money; on the other hand, I knew I was very good at spending it.

I never knew how much was in our bank account, because I never balanced our checkbook and online banking wasn't available for our bank yet. I would write checks and forget about them, they would bounce, and I would be $35 poorer due to returned-check fees.

I didn't set a budget, but only wrote down what I spent, so there was no plan on where our money was going every month. I just hoped and prayed that my debit card or credit card would get accepted when I swiped it. The only time I would actually think about our money was when the monthly bill came or when I happened to find myself in the bank to make a deposit and did a balance check on the account.

Fast-forward five years, and there I was sitting on our bed with more than $40,000 worth of debt—$42,000, to be exact—credit card bills spread out around me. I had just come clean to Mark and told him about the mess that I had gotten us into.

The debt broke down in this way:

- $12,000 in school loans
- $8,000 in car loans (from the Audi purchase)
- $22,000 in credit card debt

Thankfully, our school loans were only $12,000. Mark never took a loan out because he had a full scholarship, but I did take one to get through my junior year of college My parents offered to pay, but at that point I wanted to be independent and pay my own way. I got a full scholarship to finish up my senior year due to the fact that I was now married and unemployed.

The $8,000 in car loans was left over from the Audi purchase. The credit card bills were all my fault. I had purchased furniture, a swing set, and so much clothing, and if we couldn't afford groceries that week they also went on the credit card. I would promise myself to pay it off in full the next month, but month after month I continued to ignore the issue. Since Mark didn't help with the finances, it was very easy for me to hide the money I had spent, but he must have realized I was spending some money, because we suddenly had more "stuff" in our home. He never asked, and I never told.

Not only did we have a lot of debt, but our brand-new house was built in 2006 right before the housing market crash. We paid $225,000 for the house in October 2006, and five months later it was only worth $190,000. To top it all off, we made $1,000 less than what we needed to pay for the basic necessities plus making all of our payments on time. Even if we had wanted to sell our house to get out of that huge mortgage we were under, we wouldn't be able to cover the $35,000 loss we would have to pay the bank to release the loan for it. We were completely stuck, with no way out.

I still had my eight-by-ten leather-bound notebook, and inside it were the dates of bounced checks, late fees, and credit card bills for which we were barely paying off the monthly interest.

If Mark had been in charge of our finances, would he have gotten us into this mess? My guess is probably not. He would have been able to stop it from happening. After all, he was the person who had paid cash for his wreck of a car in college and never used credit cards until he met me.

I found myself looking back to those years of shoplifting as a teenager. Was I doing the same exact thing, but just using a credit card instead of stealing? I started to see that my behavior as an adult mimicked my behavior as a teen.

IS SPENDING MONEY ON A CREDIT CARD WITH NO INTENTION OF PAYING IT BACK ANYTIME SOON THE SAME THING AS THEFT?

I was going shopping, and purchasing things with no idea how I would eventually pay for them. Theft is taking something without paying for it; buying something on a credit card when you are dead broke is taking something when you have no idea how to pay it back.

There I sat, drowning in credit card debt, unable to pay for groceries or our monthly bills, and wondering how we would ever get out of this mess. I felt the same sting of guilt that I felt when my mom caught me shoplifting at fourteen, but this was even more devastating. I felt the same sweat on my brow as I had twelve years before standing in front of her. Except now I was standing in front of my husband, madly in love, and completely responsible for devastating our family finances. I was afraid he would leave me and I would be alone, stuck with my maxed-out credit cards. Thankfully, he didn't leave me, and he forgave me, which allowed me to move on and begin my recovery.

In the following chapters of this book, I will walk you through what it takes to become a Recovering Spender. Just as a recovering alcoholic shouldn't walk into a bar with a $10 bill, a Recovering Spender shouldn't walk into a mall with a credit card. There are certain boundaries that you will have to set up for yourself. It won't be easy, but you can do it. I know, because I did.

You'll have to learn how to budget and actually stick to it, which may seem like the absolute worst thing in the world. But I'll let you in on a little secret. Budgeting is actually a Spender's best-kept secret and best friend. Let me explain in more detail while you pick up your chin from the ground.

As a mom of four young children, I have certain boundaries for them. One of my favorite physical boundaries is the fence around our backyard. I love it because I can let them outside and they can play and be safe. I don't have to worry about them running into traffic. It is a place where I feel comfortable letting them have the freedom to roam and explore. They also feel safe because they know where they can go and what the boundaries are. The fence is there for both them and me, and the promise of safety is what makes it work.

A budget for a Spender is similar to a fenced-in backyard for my kids. It is meant for safety, not for the strangulation of creativity and fun. It is meant to give us freedom, up to a point. Think of your newly created budget as a fence around your money. The fence gives you the boundaries as to how you can spend your money. It doesn't say you can't have fun or can't spend, which is how you think it will feel. The budget fence says, "Here is how you can spend your money. Learn how to have fun within this fence."

When I first started learning how to budget, I did feel as if my freedom had been taken away from me. After budgeting for a few months, I realized that I spent money without thinking about it. I also realized that I spent money on some pretty stupid things. Once I purchased a pink plastic mirror (with a stool) for my daughters. It sang, "Mirror, mirror on the wall," and after walking by it five times in one day and hearing it play the song over and over, I realized it was a mistake. Just one day with that jeweled and sparkly pink mirror in my house and it drove me crazy. The point was that I hadn't thought about the purchase, I had just thought three princess-obsessed daughters would love it. I came home two days later to find it thrown on the side of the road by my more practical and non-princess-obsessed husband, who couldn't stand hearing that song one more time.

It took me a good six months to be able to stick to a budget and not over-spend. There were many months of incurred overdraft fees thanks to my lack of planning and inability to say no. Before the beginning of every month we would sit down to talk about our budget and break down our expenses. At this time, Mark's take-home pay was $4,000 per month after 401(k) contributions and health care deductions. This was an annual salary of $70,000 per year. At that time here is what the breakdown looked like:

- Mortgage payment (what we paid for our mortgage plus property taxes)—$1,700 per month.
- Groceries—$200 per month. (We got this down from $1,000 per month.)
- Miscellaneous money (this was money budgeting for unplanned expenses)—$50 per month.
- Gift money (we would set aside money every month for gifts, so that I could look for good deals all year long)—$25 per month.
- Utilities (gas and electric)—$150 per month.
- Water bill—$100 per month.
- Life insurance—$25 per month.
- Car insurance—$150 per month.
- Tithing to our church—$400 per month.
- Car payments—$440 per month.

- Clothing (we didn't have any money to go shopping)—$0 per month.
- Gas—$150 per month.
- Student loan payment—$108 per month.
- Train pass for Mark to get to work—$60 per month.
- Eating out (this was cut totally out)—$0 per month.
- Cell phones (we had cheap flip phones)—$80 per month.
- Internet—$45 per month. (We split the bill with our neighbors, because since we lived so close together we were both able to use our service.)
- Cable (we had basic cable, and would rent DVDs from the library for free)—$10 per month.
- Medicine/medical (co-pays and medicine)—$100 per month.

In total, after all of our expenses were added up, we had $3,793 in bills per month. Add in the credit card minimum payments at $500 per month and we were over budget by $293 per month.

In order to make ends meet, we had to rent out one of the bedrooms in our house at $300 per month. After receiving that rent payment each month we were left with $7 (if we were lucky and stayed on budget). Every single month I had to face the reality that I had a $7 margin of error. If I kept lights on for too long, or put too much gas in the car, I would go over budget. If I went over budget, that meant less food on the table or skipping a credit card payment. There was literally no room for mistakes, and we prayed daily against emergencies and surprise expenses.

Once we finished talking about our budget and had figured out where to allocate our money for the month, we would take cash out of our checking account and divvy it up. When I first started budgeting this way I would use my debit card anyway, ignoring the budget. Mark would have already allocated all of our money for bills, so we would overdraw. Month after month I kept on screwing up the budget. I would get discouraged and think to myself, "Am I ever going to be able to do this?" There were many months of self-doubt, discouragement, and mistakes. But then, finally, it all clicked. Practice makes perfect, they say, and in this case it did. Month after month, I continued to screw up the budget, but month after month I also got a little better. I was trying really hard and kept on reminding myself to "stay within the fence."

A Spender needs a few months to learn the ropes of budgeting, so it is imperative to be on the same page with your significant other so he can help you through this process. You will be in a kind of withdrawal from the high of spending money. Like an addict, you need a few months to get through that process. Find something else that relaxes you instead; take up yoga or read a book whenever you feel the need to shop.

What I found with budgeting was the opposite of what I thought I would find. Budgeting actually helped me achieve true freedom with my money. Once you start, you will easily begin to see where you failed to draw the line and what your triggers are.

Imagine knowing exactly how much money you have for everything an entire month ahead of time. Now imagine knowing that when you go shopping you don't have to feel guilty, but can actually have fun. Just because you have a budget (that fence) around your money doesn't mean you can't have fun. It just means you tell yourself where you are going to have fun and what it is going to cost you. You can take control of your money instead of your money taking control of you.

The budget fence is there for your protection, not to harm you. It is meant to tell you how to spend your money in a safe and productive way, not to tell you not to do anything fun. There are times when you will jump over the fence or go through the gate trying to escape, but as a Spender there is danger on the other side. There may be a group outing to a mall that you tag along with. There may be a brand-new Michael Kors bag on clearance for only $200 (this example is from my own experience). There may be a once-a-year clothing sale at your favorite store. There will always be something waiting to be bought on the other side of that fence, but if you stay within your budget fence you are safe. Leave the fence without accountability and you are running into a busy highway and are about to get hurt.

You will have to learn how to set up an accountability partner, use cash, limit online shopping, and change your values and mind-set about money. But all of those changes are so much better than living the rest of your life in bondage to your spending habits. I can tell you that is no way to live.

So, how does one who is a spending addict get help without going to counseling for life? I never did attend a support group, because I felt that I had such great support at home. If I hadn't had that support, I would have gladly attended. In the next chapters, I will walk you through how I did it. I will never be a normal spender. As a Recovering Spender, I have to live a life with boundaries. Those boundaries give me a great sense of freedom, and I can't wait to share why!

The past eight years have been a journey for me, from spending addict to Recovering Spender, while working my way to now being debt-free. I learned how to be accountable and set reasonable boundaries, and in the past five years I have taught this message to more than 14 million women through my website, laurengreutman.com. The strategies I have developed to help put myself in a place of recovery are life-changing. Living a life enslaved to the money you spend every day is no fun. You may love the fun of spending and getting new things, but the guilt afterward is too much to handle forever.

In the chapters that follow, you will learn exactly how I was able to stop spending, get us out of more than $40,000 of debt, and live a life filled with financial freedom. Yes, I still have the urge to shop, but I don't go outside of the fence. The fence is my safe place, and I hope to help you build your fence as well.

When in doubt, feel free to borrow my mantra: "Stay within the fence!"

PART 2

Chapter 13

The Twelve Recovering Spender Steps

I spent years and years of my life failing with money. I would try a certain budget system, use it for a week or a month, then I'd fall off the wagon and be unable to get back on again. It seemed everything I tried was meant for someone who was "good" with money. What about someone who is a Spender? What help is out there for us? I thought, "We surely aren't a lost cause, there has to be a way to help us." After finding out what was working for me, I wondered if it could help others as well. It was then that I started putting together the system I used as part of my recovery process, in the hope of helping others in the same situation.

I came up with a Spender's recovery plan, similar to the twelve-step process in Alcoholics Anonymous. This plan is meant to help people transition from being a Spender, to being in recovery mode, and finally to becoming a Recovering Spender.

You may be sitting there wondering, "How do I know if I need to be in recovery?" The signs are pretty clear:

- If you are having continual arguments with your spouse or significant other over money and are having a hard time affording basic necessities, you need to be in recovery.
- If you bought a new purse, despite owning twenty others, yet are in credit card debt and feel guilt after the purchase, you need to be in recovery.
- If you refuse to cancel your premium cable or stop ordering takeout, but have credit card debt that you have no idea how you'll pay off, you need to be in recovery.
- If you have ten maxed-out credit cards and have refinanced your home twice to pay down your debt, but refuse to get rid of your iPhone, you need to be in recovery.

There are so many more scenarios that I can run past you, but I think you get the point that if you are having financial difficulties like the ones I outlined in the previous chapters, you need to be in recovery for a chance at getting out of this mess.

That is what I did, and it worked for me and thousands of others who I taught in my online course, The Financial Renovation. This course walks you through the steps featured in the next twelve chapters. It takes you deeper into your own personal finances, helps you figure out a plan to stop spending and get out of debt, and I personally hold your hand while you walk through it. You can find out more information about the course at shop.laurengreutman.com/community. It is not easy, but if you follow these twelve steps, you will be on your way to becoming a Recovering Spender. I will be sharing case studies throughout the steps, but keep in mind that the names have been changed to protect the privacy of the people who have taken my course. You will see that not only did this twelve-step process change me, but so many others as well. By following these twelve steps, you will start to have more control over your money, less stress, and a plan to follow so you can achieve financial freedom.

It's very important to give yourself a grace period of about three to six months during this process. You need to be aware that it will take some time and practice. It's okay to fall off the wagon—it is expected at first. You simply need to get back on the wagon and keep on trucking. Budgeting and learning a new skill takes time and practice, just like cooking or learning to ride a bike. Budgeting and learning how to properly handle money is a learned skill that you probably weren't taught in school, which is unfortunate. Promise me that you will not quit!

You haven't had a successful budget yet, so how do you expect to stick to one that you just pulled out of thin air? It takes a few months to figure out the correct numbers in your budget, you may underbudget in some categories and overbudget in others. Once you have a few months under your belt, you'll start to see where you can decrease your bills and what you can completely eliminate.

You will need to learn how to set successful and realistic boundaries, which we will talk more about in Step 7. Think about it this way: Walking into the mall with a credit card in your purse yet telling yourself you are just looking is just like an alcoholic going into a bar with whiskey in her pocket and telling herself she won't drink.

One visit to the mall with a friend of mine who had a lot of money made me realize that I did not have the willpower. I somehow got lost in the markdowns at Forever 21 and came home with a few bags of "great deals." I got sucked into thinking that it was okay for me to shop because I was saving money. But we didn't have any clothing money in our budget, so those great deals cost me a lot of money in overdraft fees.

After almost eight years of doing little to no mall shopping, I can finally go into a mall and not shop outside of what I need. It took a lot of practice, and I've learned to stick to my boundaries, like not carrying a credit card when I shop.

Over the years, I've learned the art of saving money on just about everything. I've also learned how to make extra cash to increase my income. In the following chapters, I will share with you everything that I learned in my debt reduction journey.

So if you think this is for you, and you're ready to get started, let's get to work. Let's get you into recovery mode using these twelve steps.

Chapter 14

Recovering Spender Step 1: Admit That You Have a Problem

Part of becoming a Recovering Spender means taking full responsibility for the choices that you've made with your money. It means apologizing to those you've hurt, taking responsibility for the messes you've created, and making a decision to move forward.

You may be reading this book thinking that you don't have a money problem and just want to learn a bit more about how to get your spending under control. That may be the case, but there may also be more to why your spending is out of control.

When looking at an iceberg, did you know that only 10 percent of the iceberg is visible above water? Similarly, as a Spender, only about 10 percent of your true feelings are visible to others. The other 90 percent of the iceberg is hidden under the water. This analogy is often used to explain addictions of many kinds, and being a Spender is no different. When it comes to emotions and reasons why you overspend, you have to get to that core 90 percent of hidden emotions in order to truly see a transformation in your spending. You can't just fix the visible 10 percent.

The main emotional reasons for overspending that came up in my survey of 2,200 women were depression, anxiety, boredom, fear, stress, and guilt.

Here are just a few examples of how women were feeling when they took my survey:

- Depression—"I get depressed about having no money, so I end up spending even more money, then feel terrible about it later!"
- Fear—"I have more bills than income, feel like I'll never catch up, so what's the point of trying?"
- Stress—"We overspend because we don't have enough income for the family to live on/pay bills—it's very difficult and stressful."
- Boredom—"I spend when I am bored or the kids need something or for gifts."
- Guilt—"I grew up poor and never had enough, so I overcompensate, I guess."
- Anxiety—"I didn't have a lot as a kid, so I want more for my kids. I have panic attacks if the pantry or fridge starts to look even slightly empty."

These emotions are the ones under the iceberg that people don't see. Others may only see the outward appearance of how nice you look, what nice cars you drive, or how you appear as if you have it all together.

Unfortunately, that iceberg is there whether you can see it or not, so those hidden feelings need to be addressed. Let's get really real today. Do you truly believe that you need to stop spending money? If you can't answer this question, let me give you a little quiz to help you make the decision.

Take this spending quiz. Most Chronic Spenders will answer yes to at least five of these twenty questions:

1. Is your spending making your family unhappy?
2. Do the feelings of being in debt cause you to lose sleep at night?
3. Does the pressure of getting out of debt distract you from daily living and/or work?
4. Have you ever borrowed something and failed to give it back? (This can be something as small as a hairclip.) If you often borrow things and do not return them, this shows a lack of empathy related to how others spend their money. If you don't care about other people's money, how can you care about your own?
5. Are you afraid that your friends/work/church will find out about your spending and debt?
6. Do you pray for someone to give you a large sum of money to pay off your debts?
7. Do your debts make you feel bad about yourself and give you a lower sense of self-esteem?
8. Do you find yourself shopping because you feel bad about your debts, only to feel worse afterward?
9. Have you ever lied to someone about how much debt you are in?
10. Have you ever borrowed money without taking into consideration how you will pay it back?

11. Have you ever promised something to a creditor that you know you will not be able to fulfill?

12. Do you continue to spend as if you have plenty of money and no debt?

13. Do you continue to do everything your friends do, for fear of being "found out"?

14. Have you tried to budget in the past, but failed over and over again?

15. Have you ever lied about spending money?

16. Have you ever hidden a purchase or just failed to mention it because you knew it would trouble someone?

17. Do you find yourself living around chaos or drama when it comes to your money? Are you always bouncing checks, missing payments, and in a financial crisis?

18. Do you live paycheck-to-paycheck?

19. Do you have a hard time passing up a good deal?

20. Do you have little to nothing in savings?

If you answered yes to five of these questions, you are in the warning zone. If you answered yes to ten or more of the questions, you need to get your spending under control, because you have the major warning signs of being a Chronic Spender.

You need to admit that you have a spending problem to yourself before you will be able to accept the help you need. I was a Chronic Spender for years, and the result was over $40,000 of debt. Once I was able to admit to myself that I had a problem, I was much more able to accept the hard work that was necessary to change my spending habits forever.

Katie joined my Financial Renovation Community with over $40,000 in debt. Although she didn't pay off much debt during the course, her life has been forever changed. The first step in her change was admitting that she was an overspender.

She joined the community to learn how to get out of debt, learn how to budget, and to get on the same page as her spouse. Her story was very similar to my story of overspending, and she was sick of spending money they didn't have, then pretending that everything was okay.

She would often shop when she was stressed out about money, which made her money situation even worse. She would stay up late at night sick to her stomach because of how much debt she had gotten her family into, and saw no way out of that mess.

She really wanted to learn how I broke the cycle of overspending and how I got better, so she signed up for my online community.

Her journey has been really hard for her. She feels as if she is in no way done with her journey of being a Recovering Spender. During the Financial Renovation course, she had a lot of unexpected expenses come up. She felt horrible using her credit cards for those expenses, but said that she would prevail and come out stronger and smarter than ever because that is just one of the things that she learned through my course.

Katie says that the Financial Renovation course forever changed the way that her family looks at and uses money. They now know how to make a budget that will work. She also learned how to meal plan which makes life so much easier. She is eager to put what she has learned through the course to use. For the first time in her adult years, she feels as if she can change her spending habits. She finally feels hope that her spending can get under control once and for all.

Once you've admitted that you have a spending issue, you need to admit that you are powerless over your spending.

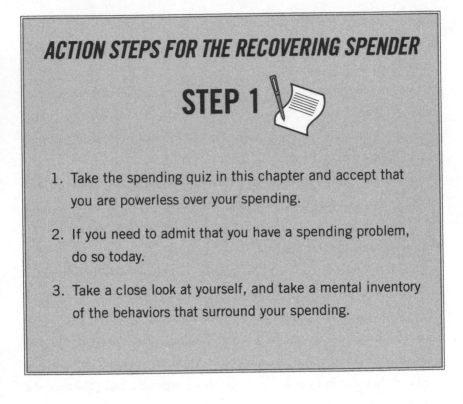

ACTION STEPS FOR THE RECOVERING SPENDER

STEP 1

1. Take the spending quiz in this chapter and accept that you are powerless over your spending.

2. If you need to admit that you have a spending problem, do so today.

3. Take a close look at yourself, and take a mental inventory of the behaviors that surround your spending.

Chapter 15

Recovering Spender Step 2:

Get Help from the One Above

Twelve-step groups have often been used to help people with addictions of various kinds—from drugs, to relationships, to shopping. I never attended a twelve-step program as a Spender but had previously attended drug-related twelve-step meetings with my brother. After leaving the groups with him, I would think to myself, "What is the appeal of these twelve-step groups?" Is it the like-minded camaraderie? Is it the safe place to go to talk? As an outsider looking in, I could see how gathering with people with similar struggles can be comforting and helpful, but what made the people stick with it?

I started to think about how helpful a twelve-step program would have been for me when I was trying to get myself out of debt. A lightbulb moment happened, and I started thinking about creating my own twelve-step process for getting out of debt and curbing spending. The major question I had was, what would help others stop their spending once and for all? There started my quest for developing my own Recovering Spender twelve-step program, a program that I created in order to help other Spenders like me.

I used other tweleve-step programs as my inspiration in the quest to develop my own twelve-step Recovering Spender system. Looking at original twelve-step program guides, there are a few similarities. One step is admitting that you have a problem; another suggests that you turn to God as a helper; and another says to learn how to make a moral inventory of yourself. Those steps are great, but where could I find the meat and bones? Where could I find the good stuff that tells *how* to do this? Certainly you can't do it all alone.

Many of the twelve-step programs mention a Higher Power. It got me wondering: Was God the missing piece of the puzzle for me? Could asking God for help really work?

I was brought up in a Presbyterian home, attending church twice on Sundays, one time in the morning and then again at night. Before Sunday morning church, I also attended Sunday school. I knew about God, I prayed to Him, and watched my parents read their Bibles every day. I didn't quite get Him, though. I would lie in bed as a little girl and pray for things like, "God, if You are real, shut my bedroom door right this second." Then I would wait, and nothing would happen. I would beat myself up about making God do something so little, but there was always that little thought in the back of my head that He wasn't real. I spent much of my teenage years going to Bible study, yet drinking on weekends. I got into a fair amount of trouble in my high school years, doing drugs and drinking too much. I hung out with the "party" kids and got in trouble with boys.

Three days after my graduation from high school, one of my friends was killed in a drunk driving accident. She was driving under the influence and rolled her car, and eventually died from her injuries. I remember having a big "God" moment then. I realized how short life was. I wish I could say that my life changed for the better that day, but it didn't. I continued to drink and smoke all the way through my freshman year of college. That first year of college was really tough for me, despite having the luxury of a free education and an allowance from my parents. I was practically flunking out and hungover every single day.

The summer after my freshman year in college, I was determined to turn my life around. I was miserable, lonely, and felt a deep hole inside. I used to go shopping because it would help me fill that hole, even though I knew about God. I started wondering if He could truly help me. During my teenage years, my mom was a leader at Young Life, a Christian outreach program for teenagers. She desperately needed a camp counselor to help her with Young Life's yearly summer camp. She needed one more counselor at the last minute, or else she would not be able to take the girls in her group, so she asked if I would help her (knowing very well that I was not following God at that time). It was a free vacation and I knew some of the girls who would be in our cabin, so I took her up on the offer. During that trip, I went to all of the sessions as a leader, but felt as if I was hearing about God for the first time. I started to think that maybe that hole and loneliness I was feeling could go away if I prayed and asked God into my heart. On a whitewater rafting trip at that summer camp, I was hit accidentally on the side of my nose by a friend's elbow. At the hospital I found out my nose was broken in two places. I had to have surgery to correct the fracture, so I wasn't able to work when I got home. That summer I sat and sat and sat. I hung out with some friends, but I wasn't able to go out in public because of the cast on my nose, black eyes, and the packing that was in my nostrils from the surgery. I could no longer do fun things with my friends, and instead had to sit on the side-lines bored out of my mind. It was then that I started to read the Bible, for myself.

I started to feel happy again. For the first time, I started to pray and read my Bible seriously, and started to learn more about God. Not in a "my parents are making me do this" way, but a real way. I had lived the past five years of my life empty inside. I was sick of all the drugs and drinking! I did a lot of reflecting that summer, and went back to college a changed person.

My sophomore year, I no longer went out drinking with my friends, but would stay at the dorms and hang out with new friends I made through the new church I was attending. This was when the shopping started to pick up, because I was bored and would often drive forty-five minutes to the mall and shop just to cure the boredom. My friends would go out to party, and I would drive myself to the mall and shop. That next summer was when I met Mark. With my rocky past, I was surprised that this church boy actually liked me for who I was and could ignore my past. Mark taught me a lot about God. He showed me what true forgive-ness and humility look like. Despite my outward appearance of continu-ing to go to church and do all the right things, I still felt as if I had a hole inside me. I knew the saying, "There is a God-shaped hole in your heart that only God can fill," but despite how hard I tried, that hole was still there.

Fast-forward to 2006, as I sat on the bed confessing to Mark about the credit card bills I had racked up. Afterward, I wondered, "Am I just pretending to be this Christian woman?" I still felt empty, and I was trying to fill the void that I felt with shopping and things. It wasn't working, so I prayed and asked God for help once again. I was also grieving from my recent miscarriage and current period of infertility. I was pretty much at rock bottom in life. I couldn't have any more kids (or so I thought), and I had gotten us into so much debt that we couldn't even afford groceries some weeks. I started attending a women's Bible study and made new friends. These women were real friends, who believed in a real God. The influence that they had on me was profound. They helped me to see that no matter what I did to fill the hole in my heart, it would never be filled unless I had God in my life.

I started learning more about God and reading the Bible in an entirely new way. Many times as I was sitting in the parking lot of my favorite store, Target, I would pray when tempted to spend money and go over budget. God gave me strength when I was weak. I was finally able to go into Target and spend money according to my budget.

Here are a few of the Bible verses that carried me through this time:

- Philippians 4:13—*I can do everything through Him who gives me strength.*
- Isaiah 41:10—*Do not fear, for I am with you; do not be dismayed, for I am your God. I will strengthen you and help you; I will uphold you with my righteous right hand.*
- Psalm 46:1—*God is our refuge and strength, an ever-present help in trouble.*
- 2 Timothy 1:7—*For God did not give us a spirit of timidity, but a spirit of power, of love and of self-discipline.*
- Proverbs 3:5–6—*Trust in the Lord with all your heart and lean not on your own understanding; in all your ways acknowledge Him, and He will make your paths straight.*

I would hang these quotations from scripture inside my car, on the mirrors in my bathroom, and wherever else I could put them to remind myself that I needed help. I fully trusted and relied on praying when I was in times of trouble, but also learned how to be thankful and praise Him when times were great! Some of these times were when I finally was able to conceive again, the day I gave birth to my baby girl Hannah, and when our house in South Carolina finally sold. I consider all of these miracles, and am so thankful that God helped me through some of the toughest times in my life.

I went from a child raised in the church, to a destructive teenager and young college student, to a young bride who learned more and more about the God she was brought up with. I've come a long way in my relationship with the Lord, and I am so thankful that the relationship continues to guide my steps.

In fact, when writing this book I prayed long and hard about what you needed to hear. I have full confidence that He has guided me, and pray that the information I've shared in this book will encourage you to believe that He can make a difference in your own life and help you make the changes needed.

Thaylor joined my Financial Renovation Community one day after praying for someone to help her with her finances. She was a Christian already, but really was having a hard time trusting that God really cared about her. She was never taught how to use money, because her family grew up really poor. They paid cash for everything and money was always tight.

Shortly after praying, she saw an announcement about my Financial Renovation Community. She signed up right away, even though she joined by charging it on her credit card. She knew that the help she would get would pay that money off within the first couple of days.

Thaylor has done some amazing things within the community. She paid off over $2,500 in debt during the seven-week course.

She says "The support system has helped me to see there is light. I am learning to budget effectively. I am meal planning and avoiding the store and the junk food at all cost! I see a future for our family now :)"

I know that God answered her prayers when she asked him for help. Because of God's answered prayers, she is well on her way to being debt-free this year!

There is a reason why twelve-step programs include steps about God. It is that you need to have something higher than yourself to call out to for help. You aren't strong enough to live life alone, especially if you are a Spender. I know that I am forever grateful for the love and guidance of Jesus Christ in my life.

ACTION STEPS FOR THE RECOVERING SPENDER

STEP 2

1. Take an inventory of how you feel right now. Do you feel there is a hole in your heart that you are trying to fill?

2. Find a list of quotes or Bible verses that help you in times of trouble, write them down, and hang them wherever you can see them daily.

3. Meditate and pray; ask for help with your spending.

Chapter 16

Recovering Spender Step 3:
Admit Your Spending to Someone Else

What is holding you back from telling someone about your bad spending habits? Is it fear, worry, anxiety, humiliation? For me, I was so ashamed about my spending that it kept me from telling Mark for a few years. I would wake up telling myself, "Today is the day," but then I would chicken out and continue to pretend that everything was fine. I would walk around filled with anxiety that he would somehow find out. That anxiety would lead me to shop, and the cycle would continue over and over again.

Secrets are known to be bad for your health, and researchers have discovered actual health benefits from simply admitting your private secrets. Let's take a look at one of those studies.

In 2012, Notre Dame professor Anita Kelly authored a study on the effects of lying. Kelly and her team worked with 110 people between the ages of eighteen and seventy-one for a ten-week period. Half of the participants agreed to try to stop telling lies during the study, while the other half received no strict instructions. Both groups were given polygraph tests, and researchers found a dramatic difference in the health of the two groups. They found that the participants who told the truth more often had 54 percent fewer issues with anxiety and depression, and 56 percent fewer physical health complaints (such as headaches). They concluded that keeping secrets and lies causes physical stress. This, in turn, causes an increase of the stress hormone cortisol to be released in the body, threatening health. The results also showed that being emotionally vulnerable paradoxically causes an increase in feelings of power, and the participants who were vulnerable (due to telling the truth) reported very little physical stress.

A common misconception of being vulnerable to another human being is that you are the weaker person; but that could not be further from the truth. Vulnerability is not weakness. Let that sink in for a minute—it is *not* weakness. As bestselling author Brené Brown (check out her TED Talk, "Listening to Shame") explained so perfectly in 2012, "Vulnerability is our most accurate measurement of courage." When secrets fester, shame increases. We are courageous when we speak out regardless of how uncomfortable it feels.

Brown also goes on to say, "If you put shame in a petri dish, it needs three things to grow exponentially: secrecy, silence, and judgment. If you put the same amount of shame in a petri dish and douse it with empathy, it can't survive."

If the shame you've felt over your spending is kept secret, it will continue to grow. If you continue to be silent about it, that shame will fester and become greater and greater. Your health may start to decline; you may feel anxious much of the day. But if you tell someone about it, you have the opportunity to kill your shame once and for all as you walk in the path of truth.

When you've confessed your spending to at least one human being, you are now ruling over that fear. You are now in control of it; it is not in control of you any longer.

Rachele was so tired of walking around on eggshells around her husband. She got her and her husband into $5,000 worth of debt in just three months. After a health care scare, she felt so stressed that she started spending money that they didn't have.

Rachele joined my Financial Renovation course with just over $5,000 in debt. She had tried to budget in the past but she had an income change which made it more difficult to keep up with her bills. After her health scare, she had to change her line of work and her income was cut in half. She joined the community to learn how to get out of debt, learn how to budget successfully, and to get on the same page as her spouse.

During the course, she paid off over $2,500 worth of debt, which was almost half! She also managed to set aside $1,500 into an emergency savings account for unexpected expenses.

Before the course, she felt this pressure every single day of how to manage money. She said that the way this course broke everything down to a manageable level each week made it so easy to tackle. The pressure is now gone and the plan is in action. Rachele is still paying off debt and plans to be debt-free within the next three months.

Rachele had to admit her spending to her spouse and by doing that, he was able to bear some of the stress from their finances. They were able to get on the same page, and work through it together. She realized there was no "right time" to tell him, so one day she just blurted it out over dinner. She was relieved when he forgave her, and offered to help.

Her life has been forever changed as she now knows how to successfully stick to a budget, save on groceries, and best of all, is now communicating with her spouse about their family finances.

I can relate to her story because when I prepared myself to confess to Mark, I sat and thought about the different ways I could tell him, but nothing seemed right. I waited and waited for the correct time and atmosphere, but it never happened. I got so sick of waiting for the perfect moment that I just blurted it out that one night. Mark was so graciously forgiving and eager to help get us back on our feet. That doesn't mean he wasn't heartbroken over all the lies I had told him.

After you've confessed, if you are able, ask that same person to help you to be accountable. This person can be the one who helps you set up your initial budget, or just calls to check up on you. Mark was my accountability partner, and it only worked because he believed in me and was a Saver.

There are times when both people in the relationship are Spenders. What happens in this situation when only one of you wants to get help? In this situation, I would suggest you both sit down and have a good long talk about it using my Financial Bucket List or the quiz from Step 1. Talk about your goals for the future and where you want your values to take you.

You may even want to include another accountability partner or join a group for help. One of the ways that I currently help people is through my Financial Renovation Community. I've gathered hundreds of Spenders together as a community to help build each other up and support each other. The women and men who are part of my community have paid off hundreds of thousands of dollars of debt, and that is due in part to their supporting and encouraging one another. You can find out more about that community at shop.laurengreutman.com/community.

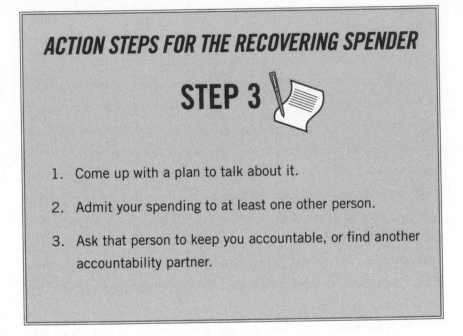

ACTION STEPS FOR THE RECOVERING SPENDER

STEP 3

1. Come up with a plan to talk about it.

2. Admit your spending to at least one other person.

3. Ask that person to keep you accountable, or find another accountability partner.

Chapter 17

Recovering Spender Step 4:
Make a List of All the People to Whom You Are in Debt

I've borrowed many things throughout my life and never returned them. This happened so often that I had to stop borrowing things because I didn't trust myself to return them. This was one of my trigger points that I found when I took the spending quiz I shared with you earlier, in Step 1. In fact, just the other day I finally returned a pair of sunglasses to my sister-in-law, eight months after I borrowed them!

How can borrowing from someone else be a trigger point for Spenders? When you borrow something and don't give it back, it shows a lack of respect for others' money. If you are in debt, you have a lack of respect for your own money, as well. When going into recovery, you need to start respecting not only your money, but that of people around you. Stop borrowing things for the time being, because when you are in debt and there is chaos all around you, it is easy to forget what you've borrowed. You need to set this as a boundary for yourself; if being in debt isn't enough trouble, remembering what you've borrowed adds an unnecessary stressor.

Multiple credit cards are also a big stressor. If you have a stack of credit cards in your drawer, you may often forget which ones have balances and which ones are canceled. In this section, we are going to work on clearing up confusion by making a list of all the people to whom you owe money. Start with individual people, but also include banks, credit card companies, insurance companies, utilities, everything!

To make this easier, I've made a printout for you at the back of this book (see Appendix B). On the printout, I want you to fill in the top of the list with your friends and family. Your first priority (regardless of how much you owe) should be to erase your debt to these people. Money can strain relationships, and you don't want that with these special people in your life. Make amends, tell them your situation, and let them know when they can expect to get their money back. Make it right with them, and don't strain the relationships even more.

To make a list of what order to pay back the people in your life, start with this:

1. Family members—Always pay them off first even though they will be the most forgiving.

2. Friends—You may want to pay off your friends first to avoid jeopardizing the friendship, but family always comes first. If you explain to them the situation, they will understand if you have a true friendship with them. Remember to give them a set date, and maybe split payments up monthly if that makes it easier.

3. Coworkers—How often do your colleagues give you money for lunch, or maybe pay half of your hotel stay at that business conference? Make sure that you pay them back before you start paying off your credit cards.

When I made that list, there were only three people in our family we had borrowed money from: my grandmother-in-law (to buy our first house and who we paid off in a few months), and my in-laws.

When my in-laws lent us the $4,000 I talked about in Chapter 8, we still had $40,000 in debt. When we finally sat down to make a list of our debts and to whom we owed money, we put Mark's parents at the very top of the list. We wanted our relationship to stay strong and were afraid of harming it by owing them money. Even though they weren't charging us any interest, our loyalty to and relationship with them was much greater than to the person on the phone at the credit card company.

Keep in mind that if you have borrowed money from family members it's best to make them the number one priority. That way not only do you pay down your debt, but you'll be preserving an important relationship as well.

This topic really resonated with Amy. Amy joined my Financial Renovation Community with over $40,000 in debt. She had never budgeted before and was very hesitant that it could actually help her. Through the seven-week course, Amy paid off over $1,000 in debt to her family members plus was able to put $300 into a savings account. She was getting really nervous about her future, which is why she joined the course. She had a lot of debt with family members, and it was starting to put a big strain on their relationships. One relative sent her money from her own HELOC (where she borrowed against the equity she had in her home) to help with a large home repair. Not only did Amy not have the money to pay the interest on that loan every month, neither did her relative. Now there were two people in financial disarray because Amy borrowed from a family member and was unable to pay it back on time.

My course exceeded her expectations. She signed up because her husband was the sole caretaker of the money, and it was stressing him out.

Amy says, "While we didn't make a huge dent in our debt, we did begin communicating better about money and began working together. We have a spending plan, goals to pay back our family members, and a working budget with financial goals. This is a first for us. We had our first budget meeting on Saturday, and my husband thanked me for taking this class and coming to his rescue. I am so grateful to have taken this class."

Amy shares that going through my Financial Renovation course was such a journey. Through the weekly lessons and challenges, she was able to find the path that leads to becoming debt-free and gain the confidence to continue on that path.

Amy as well as many others in my community have expressed regret over borrowing money from family members without any conversation about how it was going to get paid back.

I know of situations where people have lent their entire retirement savings to a family member in need, then have to work an extra ten years just to be able to pay their bills because they never got their money back. Don't be that person who doesn't pay back a family member.

I suggest that if you absolutely have to borrow money from a family member, put the payment terms down in writing. Keep the communication open, and don't let things get weird in the relationship. That relationship is much more important than money, so make sure that the relationship stays the focus.

ACTION STEPS FOR THE RECOVERING SPENDER

STEP 4

1. Make a list of your debts.

2. Make amends with family members or friends who have lent you money.

3. Focus on paying those debts off first before any other.

Chapter 18

Recovering Spender Step 5:
Take an Inventory of Your Spending

As a Spender, you probably aren't writing down how much money you spend. If you did so in the past, it may have overwhelmed you to the point where you quit because you didn't want to face the damage. You also may be making a lot of transactions and sitting down to record them could take days. But it is important that you do this in order to figure out what your starting point should be, similar to weighing yourself before you go on a diet.

Finding your starting point may be the hardest part of your journey to recovery. You start to see where your money is going, and that starts to show you your value system. It also shows you the damage that you've done to your money.

Julie came into the Financial Renovation Community with a lot of money damage. Over $40,000 of debt. She had never budgeted before and had no idea where to start. When she started going through my online course, she admitted to having no idea how much money she was making or spending. She would spend freely and hope and pray that her card wouldn't get declined at the register.

She was an overspender and was sick and tired of wishing and hoping that she could pay her bills on time. I have three in-depth videos in my online community where I show you easy ways to take inventory of your spending. I have spreadsheets and programs to help you figure this out fairly quickly. She was absolutely shocked when she took inventory of her spending, suddenly realizing that she was spending over $3,000 more per month than what she was making. No wonder she was having problems paying her bills.

After coming to grips with her spending and finding many ways to cut back those expenses, Julie went on to pay off $2,000 in debt and put $1,000 into an emergency savings account. Julie had this to say about her experience: "Lauren has put together a great plan to help others get out of debt. She is always encouraging you and never judging or shaming you for your debt. She uses very simple and understandable ways to help you get to your goal of financial freedom."

Do you want to be like Julie and take control of your finances? Here are the steps you need to take to make an inventory of your spending and learn how to make things better.

First, print out the most recent three months of credit card and bank statements and staple them all together. Next, enter each amount onto a worksheet of some kind. This will help you to find out how much you've been spending. Be sure to put each transaction into a category.

I can guarantee that you'll be shocked at how much you are spending in certain categories. When Mark and I did this the first time, we couldn't believe how much we were spending on food. Even though there were only three of us at that time, and one was a toddler with a small appetite, we averaged $1,000 per month (sometimes more). We would eat out often because with Mark getting home from work at 6:00 p.m., it was easier for us. We would order a lot of pizza, eat out at restaurants, and then go to the grocery store once or twice per week. We weren't eating at home much, so the food from the grocery store would spoil, and I would have to go buy more. I estimate that we spent about $600 per month eating out and about $400 per month at the grocery store.

Once you start writing everything down, realize that this exercise is going to take time, but why do you want it? That is what you need to come up with—the *why*—when things get hard. When you want to quit, think about why you are spending the time to track this. Paste that *why* everywhere you can, and remember it to help fuel this process.

Here are the categories you are going to use when writing down those transactions:

- Auto (car payments)
- Childcare
- Clothing
- Debt payments (minimum payments)
- Eating out
- Education (school supplies or tuition)
- Entertainment (movies, games, etc.)
- Gift money
- Giving
- Groceries
- Health care (co-pays or out-of-pocket expenses)
- Hobbies
- Household
- Insurance

- Pet care
- Savings
- Utilities
- Miscellaneous (random expenses)

Using the statements you printed out, write each transaction down in its proper category. I've provided you with a worksheet to help you out. You can find it in the back of this book (see Appendix C).

Go through every statement, add up all the categories on either the printable sheet or the spreadsheet, and then come up with a total.

Before you do this, be aware that a few things may happen:

1. You may discover that you are even more broke than you thought. Be warned, this might feel pretty depressing and may make you want to quit before you even get started. If that happens, be thankful that you know the worst now and continue in this exercise with me. It will get easier, and soon you'll see a light at the end of the tunnel, I promise. Remember, I've been there before you!

2. You may be shocked at how much money you've been spending. This is normal, and I expect you to feel this way.

3. You may discover you are actually in pretty good shape, and once you learn how to cut back on some of your expenses, you can start to pay down more debt! This is *great news*!

Whichever way you feel, just know that you aren't alone. This is the hardest part of getting started, so let's just rip that Band-Aid off as quickly as possible and get it over with, so the hurt doesn't linger.

Now that you have all of your transactions written down from all your statements, take the total for each category and divide by three to figure out the average amount spent in each category.

Here is an example of what this can look like:

Month 1:

- Food: $1,000
- Gas: $200
- Eating out: $400
- Miscellaneous: $550

Month 2:

- Food: $1,200
- Gas: $300
- Eating out: $450
- Miscellaneous: $350

Month 3:

- Food: $1,150
- Gas: $250
- Eating out: $500
- Miscellaneous: $500

Averages from the three months:

- Food—1,000 + $1,200 + $1,150 = $3,350 divided by 3 = $1,117

- Gas—$200 + $300 + $250 = $750 divided by 3 = $250
- Eating out—$400 + $450 + $500 = $1,350 divided by 3 = $450
- Miscellaneous—$550 + $350 + $500 = $1,400 divided by 3 = $467

The average category amounts are the numbers that we'll use to create your first budget. Remember, the goal of a budget is to be able to stick to it, so if we just pull random numbers out of the air, you are guaranteed to fail. I believe this is the biggest reason people fail at a budget, because they just use numbers that sound good but that have no relationship with reality.

If we were to set up your budget using the examples above, this is where we would start with each of those categories:

- Food—$1,120 (I rounded up a bit; we should be able to get this number down a lot!). I round up so I can take cash from a cash machine in twenties. This is not a necessity, but I am thinking of cash withdrawals from an ATM. If you were to go into your bank, request the exact amount of money needed.
- Gas—$260 (rounded up to an even number).
- Eating out—$780 (again, rounded down to an even number—we should be able to cut this back a lot, too!).
- Miscellaneous—$480 (rounded up).

People ask me all the time, "What is the right amount to budget for X, Y, or Z?" My answer is always, "I can't tell you that," because the right amount is different for everyone. We'll find that right number by looking at your past spending, and use the numbers we come up with to create your first budget. Over time, we will work on getting that amount down, and the correct number you should use in your budget will be lower than what we start with.

By calculating your averages, you'll be able to start a budget without feeling the constraints of one, because you are currently spending that amount of money. The first step in a successful budget is making one; the second step is actually sticking to it. Once you've been able to stick to the budget for two or three months, start to cut things out and reduce where needed.

Don't go crazy and start taking things out of the budget just yet. We need to make sure that we have set it up correctly, so hang on to these numbers and let's begin.

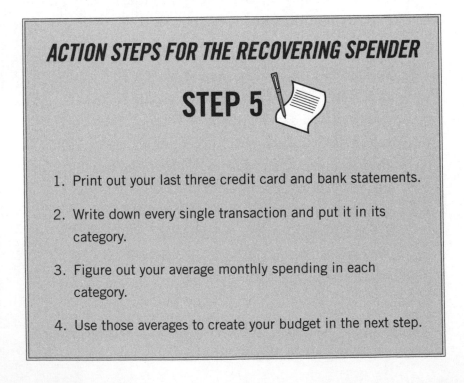

ACTION STEPS FOR THE RECOVERING SPENDER

STEP 5

1. Print out your last three credit card and bank statements.

2. Write down every single transaction and put it in its category.

3. Figure out your average monthly spending in each category.

4. Use those averages to create your budget in the next step.

Chapter 19

Recovering Spender Step 6:
Set Your New Budget

The dreaded "B-word" that every Spender hates to think about.

I'm sorry to say that it is now time for us to talk about that B-word.

Remember the chapter about how fences keep us safe? Just as that fence keeps children and pets safe, budgets keep us safe from our own impulses. That's the whole point. You want to be safe around money, right? So let's talk about how to set up a successful budget as a Spender. Remember, you will need to remind yourself to **stay within the fence**.

This budget is part of the boundary that you are going to put around yourself and your money. It will keep you from losing control and getting into a mess again.

If you are scared to budget, know that you are not alone. According to my survey, here are some of the reasons why Spenders feel out of control with their spending:

- They have too many obligations.
- They don't have enough money.
- They are impulsive Spenders.
- They are disorganized and don't know where their money is going.
- They have unexpected expenses.
- Inflation messes up their budget.
- They don't have plans.
- They are lazy and just do what is easier and faster.
- They are uneducated when it comes to money—no one ever taught them how to handle it.
- They feel they deserve new things.
- They spend too much on food.
- They eat out too much.
- They have so much debt, they just ignore it.
- It is easier to spend money than it is to save money.
- They are bored and shopping is a hobby.
- They are in denial.
- They have a fear of failing at a budget, so they don't even start.
- They think a budget is too restrictive.

Do you relate to any of these? The main reason I stayed away from budgeting for so long was because I didn't want to feel restricted. I liked spending money and I didn't want anyone to tell me what to do. I had tried and failed so many times that I felt like I was a lost cause and would never be able to stick to any budget.

I find that many of the people whom I work with feel the same way.

Many of them have tried to budget in the past b

to it. One member of my online community, N

when she joined. Mary Ann joined this course wi

had tried budgeting in the past but did it as an an

failed. She always had issues with her budget bec

liked my method of planning for the upcoming month, making budgeting much more realistic. She was able to pay off over $700 in debt and add $1,000 to her savings account during the seven-week course

Mary Ann describes the Financial Renovation course as enlightening, empowering and life changing. The step-by-step course taught her a very practical and doable approach to money management. She says, "I have read several books and read other websites, but the Financial Renovation course really put it all together in a supportive and encouraging package."

Sometimes having someone teach you what works for them can really make a profound impact.

When first starting a budget, it's important to understand the difference between tracking your spending and prospective budgeting. You don't need to track every single expense (that stressed me out just thinking about it). The better way is to budget prospectively for the entire month ahead. Brian Tracy, CEO of Brian Tracy International, specializes in the training and development of individuals and organizations. In one of his articles he states, "Every minute you spend in planning saves 10 minutes in execution; this gives you a 1,000 percent Return on Energy." You save time by planning for your month before it starts, because instead of stressing all day long about how much money you have in your bank account, you are going to have more mental freedom to do the things you love. Am I convincing you yet that this could be fun?

It's important to note that when you budget you should not be setting the same budget every single month. Your budget needs to be flexible and move around based on the anticipated expenses in the months ahead.

ink about it, different things come up every month: birthdays, days, new snow tires for the car...you get my point.

When Mark and I sit down for our budget night, we do it around the last day of the month. This gives us the time to discuss what is coming up in the next month. We anticipate what some of our activities and expenses may be. Here are some examples of questions you might ask yourself during this monthly budget night:

- Will I be traveling?
- Are there any presents I need to buy?
- Do my kids need field trip money?
- Are there any holidays when I am entertaining?
- Do I have any events for the week that I need to spend money on?
- Are there any home or car repairs I have to make this month?

If you answered yes to any of these, figure out how much you need to set aside, then write those numbers down and save them for your budget night meeting.

To make your first budget, we are going to take out those statements you printed out from the last chapter. We are also going take out the worksheet that you used to calculate those averages from the past three months. Now it's time to start putting your budget together.

The first thing you are going to do is to write down all of your expenses that are set in stone. Here are some nonnegotiable expenses that you *have* to pay every single month in order to live. These expenses are typically the same every month, so they are easily predictable. (Take note—cable TV is not on this list; you surely won't die if you don't have cable. Many men may disagree, I know...)

- Mortgage
- Car payment
- Credit card minimum payments
- Car registration
- School tuition
- School loan payments
- Health care premiums

After you have written down these set-in-stone expenses, write down the expenses that can fluctuate. You may pay $50 one month for these items, and then $150 the next. This is why budgeting for each month individually is so important. Here are some examples of what those types of expenses could look like:

- Natural gas
- Electricity
- Water
- Gas
- Groceries
- Clothing
- Miscellaneous cash expenses

Let me stop right here and focus on clothing, because this is a tough one for Spenders. We like to shop, and that could mean you love the mall and buying new clothes. Clothing is necessary, but that doesn't mean that a Spender can put clothing in her budget every month. This is one of those categories where you can either give yourself a spending limit every month (remember, you can still have fun within the fence as long as you can afford it), or you can have months when there is no clothing budget at all. Most months, buying new clothes can be more of a want than a need.

As a thrift store shopper, I write a small amount of money (around $10) into my monthly budget and shop at thrift stores on their 50-percent-off days. I still need to wear clothing, but it is important that I fit it into my budget every month and plan ahead.

Now we're going to write down those expenses that can be negotiated, and we'll talk about how to negotiate these in Step 10. Here are some examples of those kind of expenses:

- Insurance (life, home, car, umbrella, etc.)—Call a local insurance broker and have them shop around for you. They can look at the lower rates and compare across multiple companies. You don't pay them, because they get a commission from the company, and you get to save a lot of money.
- Cell phone—Look into different types of cell phone coverage. Maybe opt to go down in minutes, or get rid of your iPhone for a year.
- Home phone—Opt to get rid of it altogether. We haven't had a home phone in seven years!
- Internet—See if you can call and negotiate your Internet rates. Call and ask for the customer retention department, then ask what kind of deal you can get. Try to find a competitor in your area, and negotiate to get the lower rates they offer.

Next, we look at expenses you don't necessarily need:

- Home phone
- Cable
- Netflix/Amazon Prime
- Mail-order clubs (wine, clothing, or any other automatic shipment program)
- Coffee (bought outside home)
- Fast food
- Restaurants
- Dates
- Magazines
- Family activities
- Hobbies
- Vacations

These items are some of the hardest expenses to cut out, because oftentimes they are the ones we really want. They are things we value, and what we do for fun. Your cable bill may be the toughest one, especially with sports fans in the home. Mark is a huge football fan. He loves the Eagles, despite our local team being the Buffalo Bills. When I first told him I wanted to cancel our cable, he was shocked and upset. After we sat down and talked about our debts and sorting out our needs versus wants, he finally agreed to cut our cable for a year so we could put that extra $80 per month toward credit card payments. I was thankful he was willing to sacrifice his cable, because it meant that our spending was heading toward being aligned with our values.

Last, we're going to add in those random monthly expenses that you figured out earlier in the chapter. Maybe you have a banquet to go to and need a fancy dress, maybe you are traveling out of town and will need some money to stay in a hotel for a night, or maybe you want to buy a brand-new pair of shoes because you broke a heel on your last good pair. Whatever those random expenses are, put them in the budget. These are expenses that will change every month, which is why you can't make a single budget that always fits every month. It needs to change and fluctuate with life events.

The most important part of a Spender's budget is the Miscellaneous category. This category should just be labeled "the Spender's Category" as far as I am concerned. In order for a budget to work for a Spender, you *must* write in a Miscellaneous category every single month. This can be $10 or over $100, but it must be accounted for. This is the category that is going to give you the freedom you want and will keep you from getting too frustrated. You won't have to write down in detail what you spent this money on. This is your money to play with for the month. It's also for those unexpected expenses that come up, like a kid's field trip you forgot about, or dog food because your kid dumped yours in the toilet (yes, this happened to me). The important part is that you take this money out in cash, and once it's gone, it is *gone*! You cannot spend any more of it!

When we first started budgeting, I took an entire month's worth of our Miscellaneous money out in cash and spent it in the first two days! I've since learned to take our Miscellaneous money out weekly, so that I don't spend it (one of my boundaries). I was so horrible at managing money that the $50 we set aside for the month was gone in the blink of an eye. I was so unaware about when and how I spent our money that this was a huge wake-up call to me. To this date, I can't even tell you what I purchased with that $50. (I probably went to Target—and the rest is history.) The pain of going another twenty-nine days without spending a single extra cent was *excruciating*. I would find myself walking around a store and picking things up and putting them in my cart, then realizing I had no money with which to purchase those things. I would have to put it all back. This would happen dozens of times within a single trip to the store, and eventually I learned to stop going into stores.

This is when I started doing things to make extra cash, just so I could treat myself to a little something special instead of breaking my budget. We are going to go over how I did this in Step 11 but it was such a great feeling to earn money instead of putting us into more debt.

NOW, START SETTING UP YOUR BUDGET

Use the worksheet found in Appendix D to help calculate your monthly bills.

- First, start with your income (your take-home pay).
- Then subtract your set-in-stone bills (mortgage, car payments, etc.).
- Next subtract your fluctuating bills (groceries, gas, utilities, etc.).
- Now subtract any bills that can be negotiated (make a note of what those lower prices will be).
- Set a Miscellaneous budget for the month (if you don't have much money, take $5 out of another category, just to give you a little wiggle room).
- Finally, I want you to take a look. Do you have any money left over?

If you don't have any money left, any expenses still on your list have to be canceled if possible.

> - Gym membership → GONE
> - Cable → GONE
> - Nails done → GONE

Those are not luxuries that you can have at this time. Get out of debt and promise yourself you can get them back.

If you do have money left over, let's start saving for a rainy day. To start a rainy day fund, I recommend aiming to save $500 to $1,500.

Okay, gut check. Does this budget overwhelm or scare you? How do you feel after seeing it all laid out? Do you feel you can do it, or do you want to hide in a closet with your childhood blanket?

There is nothing to be afraid of. When I first set my budget, it was enlightening and I actually felt better. I hadn't realized how many times I would need to tell myself no. I realized that much of my life revolved around buying new stuff and being surrounded by that stuff. Once I had my budget set up, I felt a lot safer in the stores, because I finally had some sort of plan to follow. But that doesn't mean it wasn't a huge challenge. I had tried so many times to put a stop to my spending, but would quit when it got too hard because I didn't have a plan.

Not only did that plan give me a path to follow, but it also helped me think about money in a different way than I had ever done in the past. For example, if I spent four hours that week working on ideas that would save us $100 on groceries, I was a lot less likely to blow $100 at Target. Suddenly, my time invested in saving money became a way to keep me on budget and safely within my fence. Why would I spend four hours to save

$100 and then turn around and spend that money in thirty minutes? That didn't seem like a very good use of my time, energy, or money.

One of the difficult parts of this process is coming to grips with the damage you've done. But be encouraged that by working on your budget and setting these boundaries, you've just made a huge step on your way to recovery.

You can learn a lot from your mistakes when you aren't busy denying them. So take this opportunity to come clean and be honest with yourself about your spending, because denial is only taking you further and deeper into your spending problem.

ACTION STEPS FOR THE RECOVERING SPENDER
STEP 6

1. Be honest with yourself about why you do not budget.

2. Write down all expenses that are set in stone.

3. Write down expenses that can fluctuate.

4. Write down expenses that can be negotiated.

5. Write down all other expenses.

6. Make a date for budget night (around the last day of the month).

7. Create your first budget.

Chapter 20

Recovering Spender Step 7:
Create Your Boundaries

Creating your first budget can be pretty stressful. I recommend taking a rejuvenating lavender bath or hitting the trails for a refreshing run to celebrate this first step and prepare yourself for the next. It's important to realize that creating your white-picket-fence budget isn't enough for a Spender and you can't stop there. You'll need to figure out ways to keep yourself inside that fence and make healthy choices. To the average Sue, keeping a debit/credit card handy may seem like a good thing, but to a Spender it's like playing with fire. Having a debit/credit card while in a store is like carrying around your drug of choice. It is harder to say no when it is so readily available.

When Mark and I decided to make the change in our finances, the very first thing we did was shred our credit cards. Yes, I actually put them through the paper shredder. We were nervous about it at first, worried what would happen if we had an emergency. We ultimately came to the conclusion that it was more damaging to keep the credit cards than to ask a family member for money if we had a life-altering emergency. I didn't have any self-control, so I took the opportunity away. Now, whenever I went shopping, I had to have cash to make the purchases I *needed*, not the ones I wanted.

I absolutely *had* to stop carrying my cards with me, because I was just too swipe happy. I had zero self-control, and when it came to purchasing things I would often swipe my card and pray there was money in the account. Most of the time I had no idea if there was enough in our checking account to cover the debit card, and I would literally pray at the checkout that it would go through, because I didn't want to face the embarrassment of having to put things back. Sometimes my prayers would work, but oftentimes I would stand at the checkout calculating which items I needed to take off the order. It became the norm, and even though I was embarrassed at first, it became something I was proud of. Proud because I was finally budgeting.

So, after shredding the credit cards, I gave myself just two options for paying for purchases, other than checks I wrote for bills:

1. CASH
2. Prepaid debit cards

Let's talk about cash for a minute. I am talking about actual cash, not debit cards. You know, that green stuff made out of paper that we all used to use to pay for things. Remember that?

My first experience on an all-cash shopping trip was a nightmare! I had taken my cash out for the week for groceries and thought I was prepared to go grocery shopping and stick to my budget. I spent the night before planning my triple-coupon strategies, which took me about three hours. I sat in my comfortable office inside my huge house, carefully printing and cutting coupons all night. Since we had only $50 per week in our grocery budget, I worked very hard to plan my shopping lists so we could eat healthfully.

I drove to the store that morning, excited that if all went well I would be able to get $200 worth of food for less than $50. I had four different transactions planned out, and I was so excited about executing my plan! I had just had my second child, so I strapped my little six-week-old baby into the baby carrier, put my son in the shopping cart, and I was off. An hour of shopping and deal hunting later, I handed my coupons over to the cashier and watched my total drop from $200 to only $44! I was thrilled! My planning and hard work had paid off. I figured I had just made $50 per hour by spending those three hours to save $150.

Pleased with myself, I pulled out my wallet. *Empty.* I had left my cash on the kitchen counter. I had no debit card with me, no checkbook or money in my checking account to pay for the food, so I was stuck at the register penniless. I had given my son a package of Goldfish crackers that we were getting for only 10 cents after coupons, so he was munching away happily in the cart until the cashier ripped his half-eaten bag of crackers right out of his hands because we couldn't pay for them. Andrew began to cry, those big ugly loud sobs that make you want to hide behind the candy bars and pretend it isn't happening. After I told the cashier that I had forgotten my money at home, she had to dig the massive pile of coupons she had just scanned out of the register box, and I had to set my cart aside so I could come back and pay later. I was mortified.

I walked out of the grocery store empty-handed, with a crying six-week-old and a four-year-old screaming, "Why don't we have money to buy food?" I felt as if all eyes in the store were on me. I imagined that everyone thought I was a mom who was too poor to buy groceries. It was one of the most embarrassing moments of my life. Here I was trying to make good financial decisions for my family, and I had just screwed it up, *again*. But had I? Looking back, the ultimate screwup would have been if I had put the groceries on a credit card to avoid the embarrassment. The only thing that saved the day in my son's eyes was the blue helium balloon and free cookie he got on our way out of the grocery store.

As I wrangled the kids back into their car seats, I pondered what had just happened. It was a day that I will never forget, because it was the first day that I didn't give up. The old Lauren would have paid with a credit or debit card even though there was no money in the account. The old Lauren would have felt defeated. The old Lauren would have never gotten back up again. The old Lauren would have gone deeper into debt to avoid being embarrassed.

The new Lauren drove fifteen minutes to her home, picked up her cash off the kitchen counter, drove fifteen minutes back to the store, got her kids back out of the car and back into the grocery cart, grabbed her cart full of groceries, and got back in line at that same store. After the cashier rang up my huge stack of coupons for the second time that morning, and I paid her with the cash, I felt empowered. While loading those groceries into the car, I cried.

A day that could have turned into another credit card–charging disaster, pushing us further into debt, had turned into a day of rejoicing. Day by day, I was gaining confidence that maybe I could do this. Had I not set up the boundaries beforehand, it would have been just like any other day. Boundaries are your best friend, and you can count on them to keep you safe and secure within your fence.

You may have read this story and thought to yourself, "That's why I use credit/debit cards. Cash is too much of a hassle and credit cards are easier." Cash is more of a hassle, but if you are a Spender you need to learn how to handle the hassle. You need to use cash and you need to be able to physically see the money leaving your hands in order to make an emotional connection with it.

You have to retrain your brain in a way when you starting using cash, because swiping a card is just too easy for a Spender. You have no visual of how much is gone, no emotional connection to the money changing hands, and no idea how much is left. The danger of continuing to go over budget is always there if you continue to just swipe a card for every purchase.

To help myself, I set up a system where every week I would take cash out in the amount I needed. I would only take out this cash for the type of purchases I would typically overspend on, such as:

- Clothing
- Date night (if we could afford it that month)
- Diapers
- Eating out as a family (also if we could afford it)
- Groceries
- Miscellaneous

Again, you should always use cash in areas where you will be tempted to overspend. Areas that are safe from overspending, for instance, could be something like gas for the car. I've never heard someone say, "I decided to get crazy and spend $500 on gas today." That just wouldn't happen, because who has room for $500 of gas in her tank? So in instances like that I decided it was safe to use our debit card. Besides, have you ever taken four small children into a gas station to prepay your gas with cash in a snowstorm when it's ten degrees out? It is *not* fun! Trust me, we tried for a little while to pay for gas with cash, and I was so frustrated every time. I was able to find one gas station where I didn't have to prepay, but it was on the outskirts of town and it took me an extra eight minutes to get there. Usually, I tried to rely on Mark to fill up the tank in the evening when I came home, or sometimes I would run out while he watched the kids. It was an extra effort, an extra trip after a long, busy day. After three months of this, we decided to allow ourselves to use debit cards for gas purchases. It was the right decision for the family.

Now let's talk about those cash-only purchases. Every week I would pull cash out of the ATM and put it in white paper envelopes all labeled on the front with what they were for. I covered my first set of envelopes in clear packing tape, reinforcing them so that they could be used over and over rather than only lasting for only one month.

It was so helpful to have those envelopes with the words written on the front for each category. I could see exactly how much money I had spent for each category that month, and how much I had left over. It helped me make better decisions on how I handled our money.

At the grocery store, if I went over my budget and didn't have enough cash, I had to get used to putting items back in order to lower my bill. It helped me make healthier food purchases, because if I went over budget, I wasn't going to put back the bananas in favor of Pop-Tarts that we didn't need.

When I started using cash, there was one problem I found that I hadn't anticipated. I shop a lot online. Shopping online is a Recovering Spender's worst trap, because you literally don't have to think. For example, Amazon saves your credit card information and passwords, so you can buy something in one click and have it at your house in two days.

When I was a child, I would often spend a week during the summer at my aunt's home. She loved to watch QVC and Home Shopping Network at night. Way past my bedtime, I would watch those shopping channels with her in absolute awe. The countdown of the deals and how much longer each one was available made my ten-year-old self want to get my own credit card and start making purchases right then and there. I was a sucker for marketing from a very early age. Back then, you had to make a phone call to purchase something, but it's so much easier to buy stuff now. This makes shopping online so much more dangerous for a Spender.

We did find a solution for shopping online, though. In order to keep myself safe from spending too much, we signed up for a prepaid debit card and I would prefund that debit card for what my online spending budget was. Typically I kept enough money in there to buy diapers (because I love the Amazon Family program). This was a way to keep me accountable, within my budget, and happily within my fence.

Another thing I would do is stop allowing shopping sites to save my credit card information and passwords, in order to make it harder for me to buy from them. Mark and I would sit down during our budget night and talk about how much money I would need to shop online that month. Then we would put that money onto a prepaid debit card and that was all I could spend. I couldn't add any more because we didn't have any more.

In conclusion, budgeting takes a lot of time and mental energy, but it also saves you so much stress and heartache. Remember that when you do your budget before the month begins and set up your boundaries beforehand, your month should be a lot less stressful. In order to keep myself on track every day, I would do a quick five-minute money check. I would take inventory of my day, what events I had coming up and what I needed money for. This is a great exercise to do with your spouse each morning so that you are on the same track for what you need. Random issues will pop up, which is why you have that Miscellaneous category. But these morning check-in meetings are great for seeing if you'll need money for work meetings or to pay the ballet teacher. This quick five-minute checkup is a great way to ensure that you're prepared for each day. By making sure that you are prepared before the day starts, you're better able to prevent any unexpected spending.

I am a true believer in making time for the things that are important to you, and that the way you spend your time is a great indicator of your values. If you tell me that budgeting takes too much time, then you are saying that it isn't valuable to you. Trust me, when you get to the point where you cannot pay your bills and your car is being towed away, you should and hopefully will make the time!

Creating a budget and setting boundaries is a great way to care for yourself. It means you love yourself and want a better future. Those boundaries are there to keep you safe. Embrace them with a sense of thankfulness and your future will be much brighter.

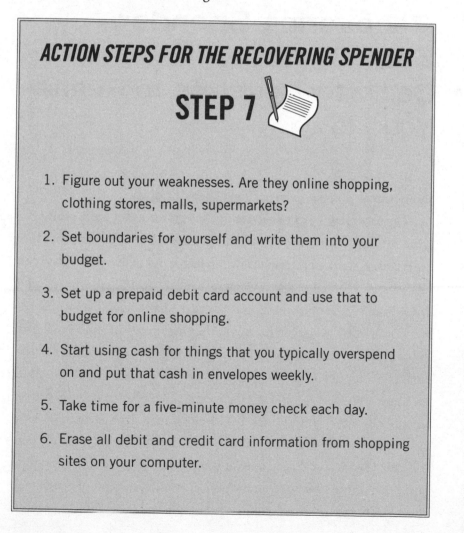

ACTION STEPS FOR THE RECOVERING SPENDER

STEP 7

1. Figure out your weaknesses. Are they online shopping, clothing stores, malls, supermarkets?

2. Set boundaries for yourself and write them into your budget.

3. Set up a prepaid debit card account and use that to budget for online shopping.

4. Start using cash for things that you typically overspend on and put that cash in envelopes weekly.

5. Take time for a five-minute money check each day.

6. Erase all debit and credit card information from shopping sites on your computer.

Chapter 21

Recovering Spender Step 8:

Declutter Your Life to Regain Your Joy

Clutter steals your joy and robs you of happiness.

The other day, I was going through my closet and it was a *mess*! I had way too many clothes, shoes, and purses. I started to clean it up, but then my bedroom was a mess from throwing clothes out of my closet. I honestly just wanted to quit, because it was just *so* much work! I sat down, staring at the massive pile of clothing, and saw that I had to come up with a system fast or else I was going to end up sleeping on top of a pile of clothes. I sat on the floor surrounded by clothes and figured out what my system would be. I would assign categories to my clothes that would help make the process much easier and less emotional since I have a habit of getting emotionally attached to things. If I loved an item, it went back into the closet immediately. If I wasn't sure about it, I put it in a pile on my bed. If I hadn't worn it in a long time, it went into a bag to either sell online or donate. The system sped up my project, and by the end of the day my closet was organized and I felt I had accomplished something important.

Furthermore, I set up future rules for clothes once they go into the closet. For example, a new shirt that I love will get hung up immediately, but then I have to take one thing out of the closet. It takes rules like this to keep things organized, because if I don't set up rules, the closet will just get messy again and I will have wasted hours of my time.

Cleaning out my closet is a good example of what it was like when I first learned how to budget. My finances were a complete mess. I had bills that were being automatically deducted from my checking account that I had no idea I was paying. I had no filing or organizational system for my paper bills, things were getting lost, and I had no idea how much debt I was in (partly because I was too afraid to know). It was embarrassing, and I didn't want anyone to see my messy room with bills and credit cards stacked high. Just like cleaning out my closet, things got a whole lot messier before they got cleaner when I first started dealing with my money. I had many nights of tears, confusion, and embarrassment as I dealt with the mess. It was so overwhelming that there were a lot of times that I wanted to quit. Knowing why I wanted to get out of debt helped me to keep on going.

It took a little time, but I finally started to declutter my finances and get my money organized and back into some sort of order. The first step was putting together my first budget, and I did it using rules similar to those I used for my closet cleanup. Those budgeting rules are necessary to keep my finances organized and decluttered. If I stop sticking to the rules I set as part of my budgeting, chaos and clutter seem to sneak in again.

After a while, the new norm becomes a clear set of financial rules. At first you have to keep reminding yourself that your hard work will pay off over time. When I first started to budget I would tell myself, "Don't look at the negative side of what I feel I can't do, look at the positive side of what I can do." A Bible verse I would frequently say out loud was

Philippians 4:13: *I can do all things through Christ who gives me strength.*
Armed with a positive mind-set, I felt much more capable of moving forward and becoming successful.

This was such a life transformation for me that the number one thing I tell Recovering Spenders who come to me for financial help is, "Clean your house." Why? Because clutter steals your joy and zaps your energy. It makes you feel that you can never get ahead.

If you want to get out of debt, you need laser focus. Money management expert Dave Ramsey calls it acting with "gazelle intensity." If you don't have laser focus, it is easy to get discouraged and quit. I don't know about you, but it's hard for me to have any sort of clarity when all I am looking at is a *mess.* Cleaning your house can help free up some of your mental space, so that you can make room for all of the new information you are about to receive. Think of my organized closet again for a second. If I were to step into a messy home I could (and would) feel drained.

I have four small children, and keeping my house clean all the time is just not practical or realistic. As I write this, I am sitting in my dining room looking at a beautiful crayon drawing on my freshly painted dining room wall. But don't let life's little messes stop you. When I say clean your house, I mean it. Give it a real spring cleaning, no matter the season. Make places for things, organize, and then sit in that clean house and stare at the clean walls. Bask in the relaxation you feel in your clean house. And when your kids leave the occasional drawing on the wall, take time to laugh, then clean it up and move on.

I was recently inspired by the book *The Life-Changing Magic of Tidying Up,* in which author Marie Kondo writes that one should go through a content audit at home. While holding up every item in your home, you should ask yourself, "Does this item bring me joy?" If the item does not, it gets donated or thrown away.

When I started to do that exercise in my own home, I would come up with a multitude of reasons why I needed to keep all my stuff. I would say things like, "I may need that someday," or "I forgot I had that." I made so many excuses, and those kept me from letting go of things. This contributed to living in mental clutter. Once I started to be bold and give more and more away, my mental clutter finally started to break up. I started to see through the fog!

When we moved back to New York from South Carolina and into that tiny town house, we had many reservations about where we would put our stuff. With the help of some men in our new church, we moved all of our belongings into our new home. One man asked, "Do you think you are downsizing too much?" I knew we were, but I didn't see any other option. We were so determined to get out of debt that we told ourselves we didn't care what anyone thought of us (but secretly I did).

We only had room for our beds, a dresser, and one of our couches in that small house. Everything else sat in the garage until we figured out what to do with it. But despite the uncomfortable feeling of being in a rental and having all of our belongings shoved into a dirty garage and storage unit, that first night in the town house was special. We borrowed a folding card table and two folding chairs from my in-laws because we had already sold our dining room set. We didn't have our coffee mugs unpacked yet, so that night we went out and bought two red coffee mugs at Walmart. We had a Keurig and some K-Cups from our old house that we unpacked, and we sat in the chairs at the table in our empty living room (which was about the size of the master suite closet in our last house). The heat wasn't even turned on, except for the space heaters in our kids' bedroom, yet the peace I felt was indescribable. I sat and looked around the dark and empty room and was overcome with gratitude. I realized that all the stuff we had was suffocating me. That stuff that I had loved so much, that had put us into debt, was now sitting in a dirty garage waiting to be sold. It had gotten us deep into debt, and I started to hate it. That stuff had robbed me of my joy, and as I sat in our empty room drinking from that red Walmart coffee mug, I was glad to be *done* with it all.

But the excitement of living so simply was brief. I started missing my old stuff and my beautiful custom house. I loved that home so much.

Our junky little town house sat in a row of run-down rental houses at the entrance to a dead-end street. On the other end of the street were beautiful custom-built homes. I would take my children for walks down that road every single day past those beautiful houses. Angry thoughts would creep in. "I used to live in one of those houses. I wasn't supposed to live in this crappy town house." I would walk by the kids playing street hockey in the road, and wave to the moms who were sitting in their driveways socializing with each other, and I would think to myself, "They know where I live, what do they think of me? I used to be just like them. They have no idea of the sacrifices that I am making in order to be debt-free."

It was as if I had dropped a social class and I was seeing things from a completely different perspective. Eventually my self-pity wore off and I would walk by those homes and wonder if the people living in them were just like I used to be. Were they drowning in debt, or were they doing all right? It's impossible to know, but I slowly became secure in the knowledge that my housing did not define me. I gained confidence in knowing that we were making the best decision for our family, and that because of this sacrifice we were going to be debt-free much faster.

Over the next two months, we sold almost everything we owned except for our beds and the couch. Mark even sold his beloved drum set (he made this sacrifice for the second time since we had been together). Every dime that we made got us closer to our goal of being debt-free; every item that left our house got us closer and closer to mental clarity. I started to feel increasingly at peace and relaxed. We were paying off debt and the space in our garage was opening up.

To realize what an impact moving into this small house was for us, here is our budget from when were living in South Carolina and had $7 left over, compared to our budget back in New York:

- Mortgage payment in South Carolina—$1,700 per month
- Rent payment in New York—$900 per month

Savings of $800 per month!

- Groceries in South Carolina—$200 per month (stayed the same)
- Miscellaneous money in South Carolina—$50 per month (stayed the same)
- Gift money in South Carolina—$25 per month (stayed the same)
- Utilities in South Carolina (gas and electric)—$150 per month
- Utilities in New York (gas and electric)—included in the rent!

Savings of $150 per month

- Water bill in South Carolina—$100 per month
- Water bill in New York—$50 per month

Savings of $50 per month

- Life insurance in South Carolina—$25 per month (stayed the same)
- Car insurance in South Carolina—$150 per month
- Car insurance in New York—$105 per month (we went down to one car for a while)

Savings of $45 per month

- Tithing to our church in South Carolina—$400 per month (stayed the same)
- Car payments in South Carolina—$450 per month
- Car payments in New York—$200 per month (we sold one of our cars)

Savings of $250 per month

- Gas in South Carolina—$150 per month (stayed the same)
- Student loan payments—$108 per month (stayed the same)
- Train pass for Mark to get to work in South Carolina—$60 per month
- Train pass for Mark to get to work in New York—$0

Savings of $60 per month

- Cell phones—$80 per month (stayed the same)
- Internet—$45 per month (stayed the same)
- Cable—$10 per month (stayed the same)
- Medicine/medical—$100 per month (stayed the same)

Just by moving from that huge house into a rental town house, we were saving $1,355 per month! That means that even though Mark had the same salary in New York as he had in South Carolina, we were able to put an extra $1,355 per month toward our debt payments.

Suddenly, that small town house didn't seem so small anymore; it felt right. We literally had no room for anything new, so I couldn't buy anything. We were seeing debt disappear quicker than we imagined, and I was seeing *hope* by reducing the stuff around me.

I started to sell items from around my house on eBay and Craigslist. Every extra cent that I made from having a garage sale, selling a piece of clothing on eBay, or selling a piece of furniture on Craigslist went to paying down our debt even more.

I continued to declutter throughout that year, and after finding out we were pregnant with our third child, we decided to buy a house a year later. We purposely bought a smaller house so we wouldn't fill it again with unnecessary things. We purchased an old 1920s home of 1,800 square feet. It was a simple home, not much flash, but significantly larger than the 800-square-foot town house. Our mortgage payments were less than the rent payments at the town house, and we were able to get approved for a loan even after the short sale a year earlier. Shortly after we moved into the new house (eighteen months after having our third child), I discovered we were pregnant with baby number four. We were thrilled at this new life, and started to talk about moving to another house that was bigger, with more bedrooms. We went house hunting a couple of times, but my gut kept on saying *no*. I was terrified of putting myself into an expensive home again. I would wake up at night with bad dreams about our money. So we decided to stay put in our modest 1,800-square-foot historic home.

I wish I had realized earlier in life that decluttering your finances and your home is *life-changing*. When I started to realize that the stuff around me was stealing my joy, it made it a little bit easier to let it go.

Now let's talk about how you can have this life-changing experience for yourself.

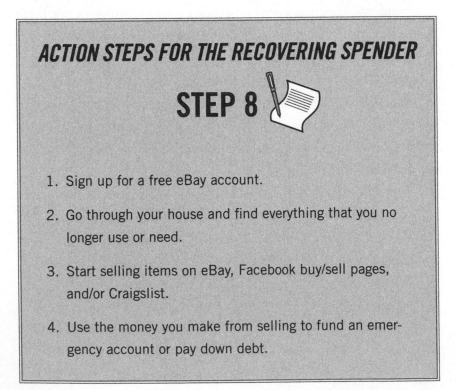

ACTION STEPS FOR THE RECOVERING SPENDER

STEP 8

1. Sign up for a free eBay account.

2. Go through your house and find everything that you no longer use or need.

3. Start selling items on eBay, Facebook buy/sell pages, and/or Craigslist.

4. Use the money you make from selling to fund an emergency account or pay down debt.

Chapter 22

Recovering Spender Step 9:
Declutter Your Finances

To start this chapter off, I have a few questions for you: Do you know how many current credit cards you have? Do you know their interest rates and yearly fees? Do you know what day your bills are due? Do you know how much money is in your bank account right now? Are you feeling anxious that I am asking you all of these questions?

The reason why you may be anxious is because all of these questions are hard to answer if you have cluttered finances. Do you think you have cluttered finances now?

A major part of going into recovery mode as a Spender is to educate yourself about your own finances, take control of what is going on, and discover a new sense of peace. In this chapter, I will walk you through the steps needed to completely declutter your finances. By the end, you should be able to know exactly what is going on financially in your life, so you can move forward with success.

1. SET UP A MONEY FLOW CENTER

One of my favorite things to say to my kids when I have them pick up their toys is, "Everything has a place." Take that advice for setting up what I call a Money Flow Center in your home.

First, you'll want to assign a designated place in your home for your Money Flow Center. I like having mine in the kitchen since that seems to be where everything ends up anyway. When bills come into your home, they should immediately be organized in your Money Flow Center. Sit down with your significant other, if you have one, and talk about how you are going to organize everything in this area, so that you are both on the same page and know where to find everything. You are going to put anything that has to do with money in your Money Flow Center. Here is what I suggest you include:

- Paychecks
- Pay stubs
- Tax statements
- Bills
- Invoices
- Checkbook
- Pen
- Stamps
- Envelopes
- Credit card bills
- Bank statements
- Coupons

Once you have a place set aside, remove everything from it that doesn't have to do with finances. This is a dedicated space now—don't let your kids color there or turn it into a place to store old newspapers. This area needs to be decluttered and recognized as being for financial stuff *only*!

Now for the organizational part. You want to grab a few things at the store—I like to have white envelopes on hand (for my cash), a coupon accordion for my coupons (you can find these at the dollar store), a calendar, and a calculator. I prefer to keep my Money Flow Center simple and place everything in a small wicker basket.

I have folders for bills, medical documents, items to file and items to shred, school items for my kids, and miscellaneous odds and ends. When something comes into the house, it gets filed right away. Now both Mark and I know where everything is and how to find it.

If you need to buy some items for your Money Flow Center, don't go crazy. Find affordable but functional options. Try your local thrift store or dollar store, recycle things from around your home. Make it as simple as possible. *Danger*: Do not go on Pinterest and search for "bill organization"; you may want to throw things at the screen because of the unrealistic and beautiful color-coordinated budgeting systems. Nobody has time for that! Put some dollar-store folders together and call it a day!

Step 1 is easy but *so* effective. Anyone can do this, even if they are organization-challenged like me. Part of my disorganization problem is that if I don't have a place for something, I either lose it or it ends up on the floor after one of my precious kids picks it up and throws it somewhere.

2. SELL ITEMS YOU DO NOT NEED AND SET UP A RAINY DAY FUND

In order to stay out of debt, you need to set up a rainy day fund where you keep $500–$1,500. If you make under $50,000 per year, I recommend saving $500; if you make over $75,000, I would recommend $1,000; if you make over $100,000 per year, I recommend savings of $1,500. You need to do this before paying off debt because you want to make sure that if there is an emergency, those expenses do *not* end up on your credit card.

When setting up this emergency fund, Mark and I opted to use a different bank from our regular one. That way we had to drive across town to get to that bank and actually walk into it to take out money. Keeping our fund at this separate bank helped us save the money instead of spending it. We tried at first to put it in an account at our regular bank, but we would tap into it occasionally to transfer money in the case of overspending. Set up your emergency account in a different bank, and leave it there untouched.

Start by decluttering your home and continue to put things aside that you can sell. There are many ways to sell your things, and with the help of Craigslist, Facebook buy/sell groups, and eBay, you should be fairly successful. I've walked many families through this process in live features on TV shows including *Good Morning America* and *Nightline*. It's always so much fun—and so rewarding—helping people go through their houses, finding what they can sell, and teaching them how and where to sell it.

Here are some general rules of thumb for selling:

- Furniture and larger items—List these on either Craigslist or through Facebook local buy/sell groups. Keep in mind that you should never have someone come to your house if you are alone, and try to meet people outside of your house as much as possible.
- High-end name-brand clothing—Sell on eBay or through websites such as Thredup.com or Tradesy.com. Brand

names such as Anthropologie, Lululemon, Michael Kors, Coach, and Athleta all sell well on eBay.

- Books that you've read—Sell these on Amazon by setting up a free Amazon seller account. Simply scan the barcode on the back of the book using the Amazon Seller app and it will show you what that book is selling for. You can choose to either ship the books directly to Amazon and they will take care of listing and selling them for you, or you can ship them from home yourself using Media Mail. Most people are able to find $200 worth of books lying around their house, so go and sell them and put that money in the fund.

- Small appliances—Do you have a bread maker or blender that you rarely use? Sell it online using a local Facebook buy/sell group. If you have a broken appliance, you can sell the parts that are still in good shape on eBay.

- Old sports equipment—Sell online on Facebook buy/sell groups or find a local sports consignment store that will buy them from you.

- Musical instruments—Mark sold his drum set and cymbals online by splitting them up on eBay. He made more money selling the set by parts. We agreed that he could buy himself a new drum set once we were out of debt.

Sell everything you can think of to help decrease clutter and free up extra cash for your emergency fund. You will be shocked at how many random things sell online. American Girl doll boxes can be sold for upward of $50 each. iPhone and iPad boxes sell for around $30! Don't think that anything is unsellable; search online and see what you can come up with. You will be shocked!

If your house starts to feel empty, you are doing a great job! All of that money you make from selling things should go into a savings account until you reach at least $500. Then start paying down your debt with the rest.

3. GET A COPY OF YOUR CREDIT REPORT

When digging my way out of debt, I was clueless as to what my credit score was or even what was on it. For Step 3, you will want to sign up to receive a free copy of your credit report through Credit Sesame or Experian. Beyond the value of knowing what your credit score is, this is a good way to see if there are any credit cards you've forgotten about or that are in collections.

When I first got my credit report, I realized I had forgotten about a lot of small store cards that I had signed up for. One of them had even been reported to collections and I was unaware of it because I had changed my address so many times. When you get your report, call all of the companies that have reported outstanding balances and pay them off as soon as you can. You will also need to remind them to put your account status back in good standing so that your credit can be repaired.

4. CANCEL ALL OF YOUR CREDIT CARDS

Any cards that you are not using should be canceled. Think of it like having an open can of gasoline next to a fire. Extra credit cards are just not necessary, and since you are a Spender, all they offer is a dangerous temptation to go out and spend again. Take that ammunition *away*.

I have proven time after time that the only way for me to stay within the fence is to use cash only. It is far too easy to spend money without thinking about it when you are using a credit card. I tried going back to credit cards once, and it was a royal mess! If you don't want to act as drastically as me by shredding them, place them in a Tupperware bin full of water, then put it in the freezer and literally freeze your cards. If you have an emergency, you have them, but it takes a while to get to them.

If you have debt on multiple credit cards, consider consolidating them all into one card with a low interest rate (zero percent would be the best). Keep in mind that this may ding your credit report just a tad, but it is worth it to have a clear frame of mind by having only one card to keep track of. Start to pay attention to the offers that are mailed to you; open them and see what the transfer rates are and what the introductory APR is. You also want to take a look at what the APR goes up to after that introductory rate has expired. You can also go into your local bank and see if there is a card that they can offer you as a valued customer.

Having all of your balances on one card will help you to *focus*, and I truly believe that even if you have to pay a little for balance transfer fees, it's worth it. The mental focus of only having to pay for one card instead of ten is *huge* and can help you mentally prepare for the large task of paying them off.

If you can't get approved for a zero percent card, call your current credit card companies and ask them if they can lower your interest rates. We had success doing this. Just making that phone call and asking works wonders.

5. SET UP AUTOMATIC PAYMENTS FOR CREDIT CARDS

What is more annoying than thinking you are getting somewhere, only to realize you forgot to pay a credit card minimum? There goes your budget, right? One thing I did to avoid this happening in the future was set up automatic bill payments through my bank to make the minimum payments on my credit cards every month. That way I didn't have to worry about missing a month and getting charged a late fee. You can easily do this through most online banking portals, and it's nice to know that your minimums are covered. I would pay extra on the cards whenever I was able to, but was also thankful that I didn't have to worry about forgetting the minimum. I would put the dates when the card minimums were paid on my calendar in my Money Flow Center, and then make a note of it during our budget night when I could pay extra on them.

I don't recommend setting up automatic payments for any other bills at this time, because you want to start getting used to knowing your expenses. You need to get in the habit of being aware of when money is being deducted from your account. Not knowing can add to the chaos. Many finance experts recommend that you learn how to automate everything, but we are Spenders so that doesn't work for us. We need physical proof in our hands so we can hit ourselves over the head with them when we make a mistake.

Decluttering is not just a one-time thing, but a new way of life. Don't think you can declutter your life in a day. I tried it, and I ended up on the couch the next day too exhausted to do anything, ordered pizza for dinner, and broke the budget. It is best to split up organizing tasks into zones and tackle them on different days. Take one day to do the bathroom, one day for the living room, and so on. Step by step and little by little, your house will start looking better. Remember that you should *not* be bringing anything new into the home during this time, because not only are we decluttering our homes to make extra cash and free mental clutter, but we are decluttering our finances as well.

ACTION STEPS FOR THE RECOVERING SPENDER
STEP 9

1. Clean up your house.

2. Set up a Money Flow Center.

3. Sell things you don't use/need.

4. Set up an emergency savings account of around $500–$1,500 at a different bank from your regular one.

5. Get your free credit report and carefully analyze it.

6. Cancel your credit cards.

7. Set up automatic bill payments for credit card minimum balances.

Chapter 23

Recovering Spender Step 10:
Do an Expense Audit

Webster's dictionary defines the word *audit* as "a complete and careful examination of the financial records of a business or person." An Expense Audit is a careful examination of your day-to-day expenses and previous records. To free up more money for your emergency fund or debt repayments, an Expense Audit is necessary.

In this chapter, we are going to do an Expense Audit of your day-to-day expenses and talk about how to reduce those expenses or possibly cut them out completely.

This is my favorite part of the Recovering Spender program, because it is so much fun to see how much money you can save if you look hard enough. I know you may shudder at the thought of losing HGTV or *Monday Night Football*, but keep in mind that we need to focus on our values, not our wants. If you are $40,000 in debt, but are not willing to cancel your cable, I want to love you enough to tell you that you have a problem. That problem is that you are unwilling to give up a luxury item for something that will mean so much more to you down the road. Trust me, I hung on to that cable box until the very last second. What in the world would I do if I couldn't shop or watch HGTV? But when I realized what $70 per month could mean to me, I was shocked.

Let's say you are currently paying $70 per month for your cable service. When your first child is born, you have the option to save for college, but decide you can't afford it. You continue to pay for cable and not save for college, and stay that way for the next eighteen years, refusing to make any changes.

Had you taken that $70 per month and invested it in a stock index fund instead, by the time your child was eighteen years old you would have saved $44,400 for his college education, making a big difference in your child's future!

Let's take a look at another scenario. You grab a Starbucks coffee on the way to work every day. You spend an extra $120 per month on coffee, not a big deal because you can afford it. If you had instead put that money in an index fund, in eighteen years you would be $76,000 richer!

Each and every purchase you make has long-term consequences, and until we as Spenders realize this, we will continue to think only about the here and now and end up breaking our budgets. So how do we go about changing the way we think about these types of things? Practice, purpose, and learning from others.

As a newly married twenty-one-year-old, I once headed out to do some grocery shopping with my mother-in-law. In the crowded aisles of our local grocery store, she went through her list and made sure to match every coupon with the sale item. To be honest, it drove me crazy! First, it took us *forever* to shop. I was used to getting in and out quickly, but for her it was an art. Being the mother of four kids, with a self-employed husband, she was always conscious of her budget. She taught me a lot in those early years of marriage, but the one thing that stuck with me was how careful she was about spending money. When I decided to learn how to lower our grocery bill, I thought back to that shopping trip and remembered how little she paid for her groceries. I thought that maybe learning how to coupon could help me cut my budget even more.

I picked up my old Dell laptop computer, the same one that had earned me my free car years before, and Googled how to use coupons. I was shocked to see that there were so many bloggers eager to share this kind of information. One glance at their blogs had me convinced, coupons weren't just for grandmas anymore. There was a new generation of young moms who were proud of how much they saved with coupons, so much so that they would show their coupon trip pictures on their websites. Suddenly, couponing was cool, and I couldn't wait to get started.

As a compulsive person, I didn't just gradually learn how to coupon. I jumped in headfirst. The first thing I needed to do was get coupons, and get them *fast*! Thankfully, there are many websites out there where I could print coupons immediately, Coupons.com being a favorite. Take one look at a website for your favorite companies and you'll see that they are practically begging you to print their coupons. I created a new e-mail account for couponing and would sign up for companies' websites to get more coupons. I would also e-mail them from their website using their "Contact Us" form and ask them for coupons in the mail. Coupons starting flowing into my house either by e-mail or snail mail, but now I was onto the next step, which was learning the art of matching those coupons with sale items. By doing this, I was promised the best deals.

I had heard about coupon shopping at drugstores. It was a complicated process, because you have to match store sales with coupons, and then use the rebates that you get from buying those items to purchase more items that give you more rebates. Here is an example of how I would make this work:

- I would buy a mascara on sale for $2.99;
- Use a $1.00 coupon;
- Pay $1.99 out of pocket;
- Earn a $2.00 rebate printed off the end of my receipt.
- I would then purchase a bottle of shampoo that was on sale for $2.99;
- Use a $1.00 coupon;
- Use the $2.00 rebate from my previous transaction;
- Get it for *free*!
- Get another $2.00 rebate printed off the bottom of my cash receipt, because of purchasing the shampoo.

I could go on and on with this, getting a lot of free deals every week. It took hours of planning and searching for the deals featured in the weekly circulars, but doing deals like this offered amazing savings, which I badly needed. I wanted to become a master at this strategy.

I took a few hours to plan my first trip, and plotted my transactions out perfectly. If all went as planned I would spend $10 on around $80 worth of items (including three packs of diapers)! I went to CVS before church started that Sunday, filled my shopping cart up to the brim with all of my good deals, and went to the cashier. I had to do this in four different transactions, and to be honest I was very nervous. My hands were sweating. I didn't have money to mess it up. I won't get into the boring details, but I walked out of that store, hopped into my car, and was in tears because that $10 I was supposed to spend had turned into $40. I had no idea where I went wrong, but I had to dip into my grocery money in order to pay because I was too embarrassed to try to figure it out in the store. Truth was, I had no idea what I was doing. I just wanted to save money.

That wasn't the last time I would leave a store in tears. There were a dozen or more other times that I would go over budget and have to tap into some other cash accounts for that month. Many times it would be our Miscellaneous fund that I would use for groceries instead. After a few weeks I finally got the hang of it, and started seeing a huge savings of around 50 percent off my grocery budget—sometimes even as much as 80 percent off!

As successful as I was at saving on groceries, it isn't the only place where you can save big money. Let's talk more about how you can save on practically everything in your life. Below are three important steps to increasing your monthly spending even more.

1. FIND OUT WHAT CLASSIFIES AS A WANT VERSUS A NEED

What separates a want from a need can be a very fine line. You need to make a list of everything you spend money on in your Miscellaneous category and mark it as a need or a want. It is really important to know this for yourself. When you pick up an item at the store, you should ask yourself, "Do I need this, or do I want this?" This will help you identify every item as a need or want.

In the case of clothing, that can fall in both your want and your need category. You need clothing, of course, but you can want clothing because you like to shop and have the latest fashions. Necessary clothing is what you can buy, but clothing you want for no practical purpose is what you should remove from your life for now. There is a fine line there, and if you don't set your budget accordingly, it can get blurred very quickly.

It was a luxury when I had any money to buy clothing, so I started shopping for much of my clothing at thrift stores. Instead of going to a retail store first, I would head into a Salvation Army store to find the $2 pair of jeans that fit into my budget. I learned when the sales were, and realized that if I shopped on Wednesdays, all clothing was 50 percent off.

Old Lauren would have been embarrassed. New Lauren loved the fact that she could actually purchase jeans that fit into her budget.

2. LEARN HOW TO SAVE ON GROCERIES

The number one place where you can see an immediate savings in your budget is on your food purchases. Eating out may be killing your budget, but it is only a symptom of a life that is unplanned. With simple meal planning and strategic grocery shopping, you can easily save hundreds of dollars per month.

Remember, in this category, one hour of planning can save you four hours of execution. Knowing that, I really started to focus on planning my meals ahead of time. Some weeks it took me four or five hours to plan out our groceries for the week, because I had to figure out a way to fit everything into our budget.

We knew we were throwing money away every week, and I knew there was so much more I could do to get that bill down. We could only afford $200 per month on groceries, so our goal was to cut our grocery bill from $1,000 down to $200 per month. I like a challenge, but this seemed impossible. I started taking that $50 per week out of my checking account in cash, and would walk into the grocery store immediately feeling defeated. I was embarrassed to use coupons because I felt everyone was looking at me thinking to themselves, "Poor girl." My pride was running the show, but I knew that if I continued to be prideful I would continue to be broke and in debt.

There were many days when I would leave the grocery store in tears because I had to put items back, or I went over budget and knew I would bounce a check because of it. It was a process, but a process that was totally worth it! Teaching myself something new was hard, but the benefits of it far outweighed the occasional failures.

I would flip through all the store circulars, matching up my coupons with the store sales. My goal was to get as much for free or as cheaply as possible every week, and planning mega-trips during the quarterly triple-coupon sales at the local grocery store definitely helped us stay within our budget. I learned to swallow my pride and was dedicated to making budgeting work despite the embarrassment of many mistakes.

It isn't easy feeding a family on only $50 per week, but I had to do it. I had to make sure that I was able to stay within budget because, frankly, it was the only money we had for groceries.

Another helpful thing I learned from my mother-in-law was meal planning, which means making a menu for the coming week. What a novel concept! The thought of planning my dinners in advance was new to me, so I had to figure out how to make it work for us.

The idea is that you plan what you are going to eat based on the sale items that week. One look at the front page of the grocery flyer tells you the best deals for the week. In fact, I learned that the items on the front of the grocery store flyer are called "loss leaders." Your store may be taking a huge loss by putting them on sale at such a deep discount, but they hope that those loss leaders will lure you into the store and make you do all your shopping there. Not me. I decided to just shop the loss leaders every week. I would make my normal weekly rounds to five different grocery stores and stock up on those loss leader sales, planning my meals around those crazy low prices.

You don't have to do this to be successful and save on your groceries. Heck, you can make just one stop at your favorite supermarket and you are good to go!

Planning meals for the entire month meant that I could stock up and save during a meat sale and prepare about a month's worth of dinners from that one trip to the store. We also ate a lot of meatless dinners, fewer fresh veggies (that was a sacrifice), and really stuck to basic meals such as beans and rice. Mark is a foodie, so this kind of diet was especially hard on him at first. He didn't like giving up extravagant dinners, but because we decided to get out of debt together we knew it would be a short-term sacrifice.

When I started my blog in 2010, I knew that one of the things I wanted to do was to help others learn the ropes of meal planning. I started creating plans other people could use and offered them to my website readers at shop.laurengreutman.com. I learned how to cook from my mom and mother-in-law, but Mark really loves to cook and come up with new recipes on a budget. He and I came up with recipes and created a system and chart that helps people make delicious recipes on a budget. These aren't just recipes, but a complete system for making twenty meals for under $150. These plans have successfully helped thousands of families lower their grocery bills, stick to their budgets, and eat delicious meals. I am very proud that I was able to take the skills I learned shopping for my family and share them with others.

3. SAVE ON YOUR HOUSEHOLD EXPENSES

The next thing you want to do when cutting back on expenses is to take a look at the section of your budget where you listed bills you can negotiate and bills you don't need to be paying.

Here are some of the bills that need negotiation:

- Insurance (life, home, car, umbrella, etc.)
- Cell phone
- Home phone
- Cable
- Internet

Below are some strategies we used for negotiating down those bills.

Insurance

One way that we got our insurance bills down was to call around to compare rates. It's common for car insurance companies to slowly increase your rate, and before you know it your $300 annual policy has crept up to $700 per year and you have no idea how. Call around and get quotes from other companies every three years or so. You can also work with a local insurance broker, who will help you get the best price and the best deal using smaller insurance companies that you may not know about.

Another way to save is to bundle your insurance products together for an even lower rate. I am a *huge* proponent of having life insurance, no matter how broke you are! For only $20 per month, you can go to bed at night knowing that your family will be taken care of financially, at least in part, if something were to happen to you.

Phones

When it comes to home phones, do you really even need one? Maybe you did back in 1990, but in 2016 most people do not have home phones. That was one of the first things we canceled when we began to be serious about getting out of debt. We chose to use only cell phones. If you're nervous about not having a phone at home with your babysitter or kids, consider purchasing a TracFone from Walmart, get a prepaid card loaded on it, and use it only when needed. A concern I had about just using a cell phone with a long-distance area code is my kids having to memorize a ten-digit phone number. To combat this, we easily set up a Google Voice phone number with a local area code. Now when people call that number it forwards to my cell phone. That way the phone number will be a local area code and stay the same all the time. If I were to change my cell phone number, I could continue to have my kids call the Google Voice number (which you can get for free through google.com/voice) and they wouldn't have to memorize a new number.

If you already have a smartphone, you don't have to get rid of it. But do your research. There are other options out there, like Republic Wireless, where you can get 2 GB of data for only $40 per month, or 1 GB of data for only $25. Plus, if you don't use all the data, they give you a refund each month. Consider calling your provider and seeing if your employer offers a corporate discount for your cell phone plan, or if there are any other discounts available to you. When Mark was working as an actuary, his profession got us a discount on our cell phone bill.

Currently, we have six people on our cell phone plan for our iPhones. My brothers-in-law and their wives are on our plan, and we split the bill evenly among our three families. This saves us around $30 each month—a nice chunk of change!

Cable and Internet

Last, when it comes to Internet service, there are so many ways to save. You can ask for a new rate using a competitor's lower rate in the area, or you can call your cable company and see if you can bundle products together for a lower rate. A friend of mine called and was able to get upgraded from basic cable and lower-speed Internet to full digital cable and high-speed internet for $20 less per month. You just have to ask.

Next, let's look at those expenses you don't have to be paying for. Here is what we did with these bills. If you are willing to do the hard work to get out of debt, you should consider doing the same.

- Home phone—Canceled. Savings of $30 per month.
- Cable—Canceled. Savings of $70 per month.
- Netflix/Amazon Prime—Split the price with two brothers-in-law. Savings of $6 per month.
- Restaurants—Didn't eat out.
- Dates—We would put our son down at a friend's house and take a walk or go sightseeing. Anything that required little to no money.
- Magazines—Didn't buy them.
- Family activities—A lot of free activities, including playgrounds and hanging out with friends.
- Hobbies—We didn't do them because we would rather pay off debt.
- Shopping trips—Trips to the mall were painful for me, so I cut them out.
- Going out with friends—I would only go if there was enough money in our Miscellaneous cash envelope.

Cutting expenses for things you love may leave you with a bit of a hole in your life. To make up for what you miss, try to develop new interests that don't cost much, and these activities may actually help you make extra money or save more down the road.

One way I would get motivated to cut back and cancel things was to think of the savings as an hourly wage. For example, if I spent two hours planning meals and grocery shopping for the week and saved $70 using coupons, that equaled a paycheck of about $35 per hour. That is much more than I could make anywhere else! I started to see other things in this way as well; when we canceled cable, phone, and Netflix, we saved $106 per month! Multiply that by twelve and I had earned an extra $1,272 that year for my family by spending about twenty minutes making phone calls. I would say that is a great hourly wage!

By doing this Expense Audit, you can usually free up a couple of hundred dollars per month to either put in your emergency fund or pay down debt. Start thinking about the possibilities and you'll find money in your own budget that you never knew was there.

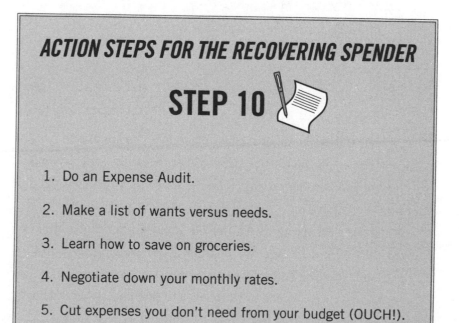

ACTION STEPS FOR THE RECOVERING SPENDER

STEP 10

1. Do an Expense Audit.

2. Make a list of wants versus needs.

3. Learn how to save on groceries.

4. Negotiate down your monthly rates.

5. Cut expenses you don't need from your budget (OUCH!).

Chapter 24

Recovering Spender Step 11:
Get Out of Debt Now!

The rich rule over the poor, and the borrower becomes the lender's slave.

—Proverbs 22:7

Have you ever thought about the fact that when you are in debt, you are a slave to the person you owe the debt to? Let that sink in for a minute... This may be more evident to you if you've ever had a car repossessed or your home foreclosed on.

When we were trying to sell our big house in South Carolina, we realized this more than ever. We thought about walking away and letting the bank take the house. There were times when we didn't see any other option. We were owned by the bank, and no matter what we did, we couldn't get away from that fact.

When we finally sold that house, we were so relieved. The house that was suffocating us had finally sold! I would not be a slave to the house any longer! It felt as if a nightmare was over.

Perhaps you may be in a house that is underwater, and you don't see how you will ever get out. You don't see hope yet. What you've read about in this book will change your life. You don't have to be a slave to the lender or to your house anymore.

Debt can feel as if it's strangling you so much that you feel stuck. I lived under that feeling for years, but developed a strategic way to pay it down.

Let's talk about two strategic steps you need to do to pay off your debt once and for all.

1. PRIORITIZE WHAT DEBTS TO PAY OFF AND WHEN

There are so many different ways to prioritize which debt to pay down first, with many finance experts disagreeing on the best way. Some say to pay off the highest interest rate first, others say to pay off the lowest balance first. I am stuck somewhere in the middle. I understand both sides, but I also realize that there are many different scenarios.

Here is what we did. We paid off the lowest balances first, which were our small store cards that were below $500. We then consolidated the rest of our smaller cards into a zero percent card. This gave us a year at no interest to start making some big strides toward paying off that balance. We still had one large card left, so we kept that one for last. If you are wondering which method will work for you, we created a spreadsheet to test the different scenarios to help you answer that question. According to my calculations, they all ended up with you paying the balances off in relatively the same amount of time. Most examples that we tested had a difference of a month or two—meaning if you paid off the highest interest rate first, you would pay the others off one month before the lowest balance.

Below is an example of the difference between paying off the smallest balances first versus the highest interest rate. We laid out the debts, with their interest rates, in the table below. If you had an extra $200 per month to add to your debt payments after paying the minimum payment, you would pay off your debt in half the time.

You can see how by paying off the debts with the highest interest rate first, you will pay off your debt one month faster, and pay $294 less over the course of the loan.

Debts	Balance	Interest Rate	Minimum Payment
Credit card	$1,300	13.00%	$30
Student loan	$16,500	8.00%	$200
Student loan 2	$3,000	6.50%	$50
Car 1	$9,000	7.00%	$250
If you only paid minimums:			10y, 7m
Number of years to debt freedom:			
Total amount paid:			$41,823
If you used an extra $200 a month:			5y, 2m
Paying off balances with the highest interest rate first:			
Number of years to debt freedom:			
Total amount paid:			$35,716
Paying off the smallest balances first:			5y, 3m
Number of years to debt freedom:			
Total amount paid:			$36,010

But there is an important difference between the two. In both scenarios, the $1,300 credit card will be paid off in the first six months. However, the scenarios differ quite a bit after that. If you pay off the debts according to the highest interest rate first, you will be carrying three pieces of debt all the way into the fourth year. If you pay off the debts by the smallest balance first, you will get that smaller student loan paid off in less than eighteen months, and then you are down to only two debts. Halfway through year three the car is paid off, and then you are only attacking that last debt.

It's those little wins along the way that keep the momentum going, and it's hard to feel like you are winning when you are still hanging on to three out of four debts into your fourth year of paying down debt. As you can see in the chart below, it is visually and mathematically not much different.

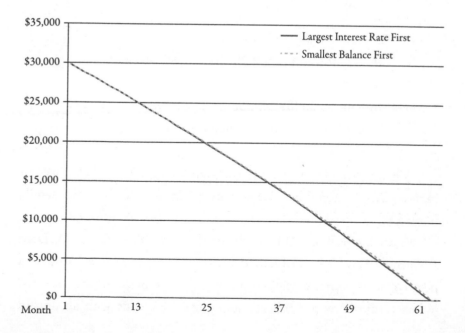

The main difference is the mind-set, and if there is one thing that you've learned throughout this book, it is that the mind is a crucial part of winning the battle.

Two questions that I typically get, both of which are equally important, are, "What if I can't afford to make my minimum payments?" and "How do I stick to a budget when I don't make enough money?"

If you are not currently making enough money to pay your bills, you should prioritize based on what you need most for survival. These types of bills include those for clothing, food, shelter, and heat and electricity. Don't pay your credit card minimum before you buy your groceries. Once you have paid for all the necessities, then start looking at your debts and pay them in the order of lowest balance to highest balance.

This is the order that Mark and I paid down our debts, and it made the most sense to us:

1. Personal loans.
2. Credit cards (starting with the lowest balance).
3. Car loans.
4. Student loans. (Remember to pay these on time, since they can garnish your wages if you don't.)

When debt collectors start to call you, just calmly tell them that you cannot pay this month because you are going to be feeding your family instead.

In an interesting 2014 article in the *New York Times*, "A Debt Collector's Day," Jake Halpern discussed his experience working at a debt-collection office as part of an investigative piece on the industry. When creditors cannot collect money from someone with an unpaid account, they sell them for pennies on the dollar to third-party debt collection companies. Halpern said that the collectors at his office "tend to be young men, often with troubled pasts." These debt collectors are out for blood, because their money is on the line and they have to get it back. Halpern wrote, "It is middle-class and poor people, being pitted against even poorer people, to the benefit of much richer people."

Something is very wrong with this system. But if you have debts, it is your responsibility to pay your bills. As a Spender, it was easy for me to ignore them and wish them away, but I always felt the sting of guilt. I knew that I had to pay them off, because I had gotten into that mess.

2. MAKE EXTRA CASH TO PAY DOWN DEBT FASTER

There are so many ways to make extra cash that are right under your nose. I started taking online surveys for companies that would pay me for my time with a check in the amount of $3. I would save that check until I didn't have any money left in our Miscellaneous budget, then take it to the bank and cash it. The cashier may have thought I was batty for being excited over a $3 check, but to me it was worth so much more. I would take that $3 in cash, go to Dunkin' Donuts with my son, and get a $2 coffee for me and a donut for him. It was a small luxury that was worth far more than the $3 cash it took to purchase. It meant that I was truly changing as I made sacrifices to better our financial future.

I definitely didn't get rich taking surveys, but it helped make me a few hundred dollars extra per year. While sitting down and watching TV at night, I would have my laptop open and take those silly ten- to fifteen-minute surveys online.

Some of my favorite companies were:

- Swagbucks
- Opinion Outpost
- Pinecone Research
- InboxDollars
- MySurvey

I would also drive to marketing research offices and participate in focus group studies. I would sit in a room with a double glass wall along with a dozen other participants and earn $100 for doing so. One time I got paid for eating two different kinds of Chinese food. Another time I had to have a discussion about my religious beliefs and how I felt about using antibiotics in commercially raised chickens. I enjoyed these experiences, and it helped us pay down our debt faster.

With so many people working full-time online, there is a huge demand for professional virtual assistants. I employ four stay-at-home moms in my business, and they get to work from home and enjoy being around their kids. I would highly recommend looking into working online as a virtual assistant, taking at-home online surveys, or looking for another type of online job. Due to my experience, I always warn about pyramid and direct sales companies. The first-level customer for these types of companies is the consultant. They try to sell to you first, then you sell to your customer. If you are a Spender, I do not recommend you join one of these companies. It is just too dangerous for you.

As a Spender, that rush you felt when spending can be transformed into a new type of rush from earning money. Not that I suggest replacing one addictive behavior with another, but I am talking more about where your focus should be. There are so many programs available to make a little extra, and when added up they can mean a lot of extra money.

One married couple, Ruth and David, joined my course together. They had over $40,000 in debt and joined the course to learn how to get out of debt and meal plan. They had tried to budget before, but were so overwhelmed by medical bills that they gave up. Due to a huge medical crisis, one of them lost their job and their medical bills grew out of control. In the seven weeks going through my Financial Renovation course, Ruth and David paid off over $9,000 in debt and put over $1,000 in an emergency savings account.

They learned not only how to save money, but also how to make extra money. They stopped seeing themselves as "stuck" in their current financial situation, and started seeing new opportunies.

They learned how to sell the things around their house on eBay and were able to make an extra $4,000 to pay down debt.

They said that "the real power of the course is the personal connection you make with us. You're just a normal person saying commonsense things, but seeing how you did it and relating to your experience is inspiring. It kept us invested in the program. Whenever a question comes up on our finances we don't necessarily see eye to eye on, we ask, what would Lauren say?"

Ruth and David see a bright financial future for their family. They continue to budget and meal plan, and are paying off more and more debt every single month.

Be like Ruth and David. Do not be a slave to your lender any longer. Once you become debt-free, you will have options and freedom you never dreamed of. Focus on that as you work toward this happy goal.

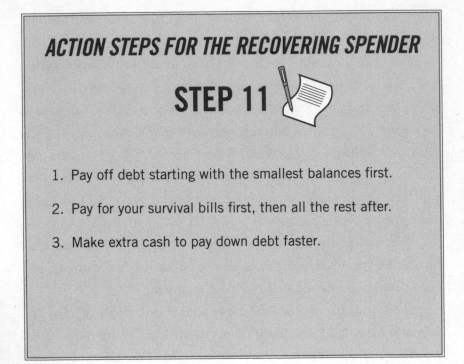

ACTION STEPS FOR THE RECOVERING SPENDER

STEP 11

1. Pay off debt starting with the smallest balances first.

2. Pay for your survival bills first, then all the rest after.

3. Make extra cash to pay down debt faster.

Chapter 25

Recovering Spender Step 12:

Curb Your Spending and Define Your Values

I have two questions for you. Right now. *Stop* reading and write down your answers.

What are you chasing in life?

What do you value in your life?

Your spending is a reflection of your values, and until you know what those values are, you will continue to spend money opposite to what you hold dear.

If you were chasing financial freedom, you certainly wouldn't be having an issue with spending. Are you chasing a better life for your family? Are you keeping up with the Joneses? Are you chasing fame?

What would financial success ultimately look like to you? Would achieving that financial success involve your changing something in your life? Could you chase what you are chasing right now and still achieve financial success?

I asked myself this question back when I calculated all of our debts.

It was painful, and it took me a while to figure it out, but I ultimately decided I was chasing the idea of being able to do whatever I wanted with our money.

Six months ago, on a special outing to the mall, we surprised our four kids with a trip to Build-A-Bear. We let them stuff their own bears, but they had to choose from the bears that were on sale. We were on a budget and told them this was all we could afford, and we couldn't buy clothing for the bears this time around. My son got very upset because his Minion stuffed bear " 'needed" a pair of overalls, which would have cost an extra $15. I showed him how much a pair of new overalls cost at the Build-A-Bear store, and then I showed him what a used pair would look like if we bought them online for $3 he had at home. I told him that if he wanted to buy them online with his own money, I would help him place his order. He wasn't interested, because he wanted them right then. I stuck to my guns and he did not walk out of that store with overalls for his Minion. And you know what happened? As soon as he left the store and we were on our way home, he realized he didn't need the overalls.

On one other occasion, I took my son to T.J. Maxx with his allowance money. He wanted to buy a Sonic race car he'd seen when we were there earlier in the week. We looked at the price tag and he was $1 short. He asked me to lend him the money and said he would pay me back when he had more. I thought about it for a minute. I had to make a decision to either be his "credit card" or show him what hard work looked like. I told him that I would not lend him the money, but I would take him home and let him do a chore for $1 instead.

My son is the oldest of our four children, and is followed by three sisters, all born within four years of each other. Taking him home instead of lending him the money was a very big inconvenience for me. I had to get all four kids back into the car, and then into our house. I had him do his chore, then got all the kids back into their coats and back to the store thirty minutes later. I had to consider the bigger picture, though, and the best possible scenario was that he would learn the importance of hard work.

For his chore he cleaned our entire backyard. I gave him his $1, we headed right back to the store, and he purchased his race car. He felt good about what he had accomplished that day.

I wonder, how often are we stealing the satisfaction of a job well done from our children by giving them whatever they want? How often are we stealing this from ourselves? When we buy whatever we want, whenever we want it, are we robbing ourselves of the joy of saying no? Are we robbing ourselves of that feeling of a job well done?

Spending begets spending, and saving begets saving. The definition of *beget* is "to bring about." In my own life, this is the truth. When I am in the spending mode, it brings about more spending. When I am in the saving mode and have myself on a strict budget, I tend to be more of a saver and make better decisions.

Why is it so hard to stop overspending? Why did I always find myself in the same exact spot where I had been in previous years? Those are questions that I frequently asked myself while in the vicious cycle of getting out of debt, then getting right back into debt. I couldn't just stop spending money. I needed to eat and put gas in my car. Why did this seem so hard?

If you don't stop spending money, it just leads to more money spent. If you were to start saving money instead, your savings would bring about more savings.

Make this the time that you curb your spending once and for all, so that you can finally stop falling prey to whatever you have been chasing.

Let me end this chapter by addressing the statement "Money doesn't buy happiness." Actually, I believe that's not true. Money can buy you happiness—if you are spending it in the right places. In a 2012 TED Talk, Michael Norton, a professor at the Harvard Business School, talks about "How to Buy Happiness." In the talk he explains his research on money and happiness, and how the two correlate. What he found is that when people give money away, they are happier than when they spend it on themselves.

Maybe you've just been spending money the wrong way. The next time you have an urge to go shopping, why don't you go out and buy something small for someone else? I think that will make you happier in the long run, and everyone benefits.

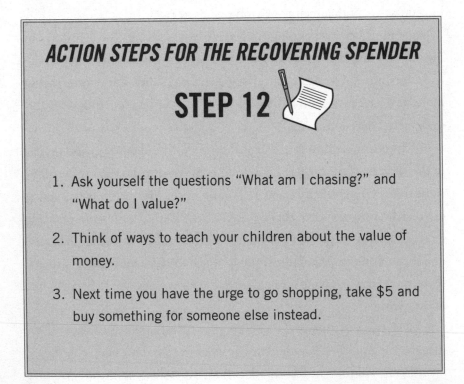

ACTION STEPS FOR THE RECOVERING SPENDER

STEP 12

1. Ask yourself the questions "What am I chasing?" and "What do I value?"

2. Think of ways to teach your children about the value of money.

3. Next time you have the urge to go shopping, take $5 and buy something for someone else instead.

Chapter 26

The Credit Card Experiment

During the writing of this book I decided to do a little experiment. I took myself off a budget for three months and made myself start using a credit card again. I'd been successfully budgeting for more than seven years, and had successfully paid off over $40,000 in debt and half of our mortgage. People around me consider me very good with money, and I agree with them; I am very good with sticking to a budget. I know my boundaries and how to stay within the fence. (Remember, I wasn't always this way.) But I wanted to see what would happen if I took myself off a budget, stopped using cash, and used a credit card instead. I haven't owned a single credit card in years, ever since we put ours through a paper shredder. I've been using cash for most of the past seven years, so using a credit card again was way outside of my comfort zone.

The first thing I did was to sign up for a card that would give me a certain amount of points if I spent $3,000 in the first three months of using it. I then stopped using cash and decided to only use the credit card for those three months. My goal was to earn enough points for a free stay at a hotel for a fun vacation for my family. I wanted to see how quickly my money rules would go out the window and I would turn back into a Spender.

In the first week I did pretty well. I didn't spend too much unnecessary money. I did try to find different ways to spend money using the credit card so that I could earn extra points. I paid a few of my bills with the card and paid them off right away online. I figured this couldn't be bad. Two nights that week I had nightmares in which I woke up in a panic attack. The nightmares were about moving back into our old house in South Carolina, and they were both the same: We decided to return to our old home and found it was back on the market, so we bought it again. I saw my family of six living in the same house where we had lived in during those stressful years. Not only were we back in that house, but we were also again in $40,000 worth of debt. Those dreams felt so real. They were the kind where you wake up and your heart is beating fast and you aren't sure if you are awake or asleep. I woke up in my current house, thankful that it was only a dream. There was no way I wanted to go back to that old way of life.

Looking back, I see those dreams as a warning. Both times I woke up mid-dream in a panic attack that we were going to go back into debt. I was terrified of using the credit card again. It literally was giving me nightmares, and I found myself *hating* what I was doing. I could see myself going down the same path again, and I was terrified. I never want to go back to that place of no self-control, transferring balances to zero percent credit cards to stay afloat, and constantly stressed because we didn't have the money for basic essentials.

At this point, I wanted to quit my experiment; it was just too hard for me to go back to old habits. Ultimately, I decided to stick it out, because the question of whether I would fall back into my old spending habits had not been answered yet.

One day I was having a rough time with the kids. I looked at Mark and said, "Can I just go somewhere by myself for an hour?" Being the great husband that he is, he put the kids to bed and I left the house to find something to do. I live in a small town and there isn't much open in the evening, so I did what most people do and headed to Walmart (it would have been Target if I had one nearby). I found myself walking around the store, sick to my stomach and anxious, looking around for something to "do" and something to buy. I picked up a York Peppermint Patty, a new curling iron, and some fake eyelashes (a total impulse purchase). I was sad, depressed, and feeling totally lost. I found myself wandering around the brightly lit store without a plan or goal. It was a very lonely feeling, but I realized that living without a budget made me depressed. I had no idea how much money was in our checking account. It felt horrible! Ironically, that feeling of depression over not knowing what was going on led to more spending because of boredom.

At the end of my experiment, three months later, I was a complete mess. I had spent $3,000 on the credit card but paid it off in full every month. Yet I had somehow managed to spend an extra $2,000 on that card and didn't know where the money had gone or what I had spent it on. I was anxious because I had no idea what we had in our bank account, and I was stressed out to the max. Here I was, seven years later, sitting on that same bed in our much smaller master bedroom. I knew that if I continued to use credit cards this way, I could end up dead broke again.

This was a huge milestone for me in my journey to financial independence. I realized that I will never "arrive" at being good with money. I will forever be in "recovery" as a Spender, and one of the things that I need to continue to do to keep myself in recovery is to stay within my fence. I know that staying inside the fence works for me. I know that if I use cash and set a budget with Mark, I stick to it and feel safe. I don't know why I always try to play with fire, but whenever I do, I certainly get burned! As a well-known expert in the field of frugal living, it's hard to admit that I still have the ability to overspend. But how helpful would I be if I said I was perfect? A common reason that Spenders continue to spend is that you lie to yourself—you tell yourself that you can stop spending, but the spending continues. You feel out of control, and that feeling leads you to spend more, and you continue to feel out of control.

If I were to tell you that I have it all figured out, I would be defeating the entire purpose and message of this book. I know that I will always be a Spender, but after seven years of successful budgeting and not owning a credit card, I thought I was strong enough to have one. The reality is that I am not, and I'm not sure I ever will be. But what I do know is that if I set a budget and make sure I am safe within my fence—I do *amazingly* well! I got us into over $40,000 worth of debt, and I got us out of over $40,000 worth of debt. I got us in debt by using credit cards, and I got us out by *not* using credit cards.

I decided to run this experiment on myself to see if I am strong enough to live outside the fence, to see if so many years of good financial habits had changed me. Unfortunately, the conclusion is that despite my excellent financial habits and new ways, it's dangerous to reintroduce some of my old temptations, because I fall right back into my old ways. This is why this book is called *The Recovering Spender* and not *The Recovered Spender*. To be in recovery, you must constantly be trying to better yourself. If I were recovered, I would be able to use a credit card and not overspend. I am in recovery, which means that I am in a constant state of trying to better myself and improve my spending habits. I realize that one bad turn can lead me down a road that I do not want to travel. One bad financial move can turn into a financial disaster for anyone who is a Recovering Spender like I am.

If you find something that works and helps you stay inside your fence, by all means continue doing it! Despite how much time you've been inside your fence, there is always danger on the other side. I much prefer to stay within my fence, stay out of debt, be happy and financially fulfilled by keeping a budget, and live the rest of my life as a Spender in recovery.

Chapter 27

Welcome to Recovery!

Growing up, I remember riding my bicycle in the driveway with my brother and sisters. I had a pink Huffy bike with a white basket in the front and pink streamers coming off the sides of the handlebars. It was every little girl's dream! Our house was up on a hill with a long, steep driveway.

I remember scribbling notes and pretending to write in cursive when I was a little girl, before I even really knew what cursive was. I would do this every day, and it would give me a sense of accomplishment. I loved folding up my piece of paper and putting it in the white basket on my pink bicycle. I would ride around for a bit, then take the piece of paper out and read the directions that I had scribbled on it. I started doing this at the age of five and continued to do it until I could actually write in cursive.

You may be saying to yourself, "Cute story, but what does it have to do with being a Spender?" Because of this journey I've taken, I realized that I am a person who likes to have things mapped out. I like to know where I am going, and I don't like getting or being lost. I really *hate* getting lost, and not just in the physical sense, but also in the sense of not having a plan in my life. I am still like that little girl writing out make-believe directions for a journey on a pink bicycle.

My favorite subjects in school were math and science, because they had a definite answer. I like to know with 100 percent certainty that I am either right or wrong. As far back as I can remember, I've been an all-or-nothing person. I give it 100 percent or I just don't do it. If I don't think I can be the best, I forget about it and move on to the next thing.

This is a good character trait when it comes to losing jobs or getting my feelings hurt, because I don't think much about it and just move on. It also helped me develop a fearless attitude about life. I want to live life, not just sit passively and let life go by. I tend to be impulsive, because I don't want to take the time to think things through.

Being an all-or-nothing person becomes a bad thing when it comes to doing something that I don't enjoy (like dishes or laundry). It also is incredibly bad when it comes to finances.

For years when I was spending money and getting us into tens of thousands of dollars' worth of debt, I was in the nothing phase of my attitude toward money. I had no map in my bike basket, I had no goals, no determination, no idea what I was doing.

You might be in the same spot in your life, or have the same type of personality. If you don't, you probably know someone who does.

Sit down and think about where you want your money to go tomorrow, next year, ten years from now. Be inspired, give it your *all*, and work hard toward achieving those goals.

I've used the Spender's recovery road map that I've laid out for you in this book for years. As shown by my credit card experiment, if I try to take a detour or go outside of my fence, I get in trouble. I like to stay within my fence, my safe place, and I can be happy and healthy there.

SO, WHAT DOES A RECOVERING SPENDER LOOK LIKE?

A Recovering Spender is someone who once caused a lot of financial strain in her family, but managed to learn more about herself. It is someone who has become very aware of her strengths and weaknesses, and of the boundaries needed to keep her in recovery.

It is someone who wants a better future for her family. A Spender in recovery is someone who cares more about others than she does about herself. It is someone who is passionate, kind, and loving. It is someone who wants to make a difference in the world.

A Recovering Spender learns to think creatively and loves financial challenges.

One of my favorite stories from my recovery journey is when we finally saved up enough money to afford new windows for our old home. They were going to cost around $8,000 and we were going to pay for them in cash at Lowe's. I had this crazy idea that we could buy gift cards from our local grocery store to earn gas points. I figured that if we purchased $8,000 in Lowe's gift cards from that store, we would earn six free tanks of gas. That would put an extra $240 back into our budget.

I went to my local grocery store to purchase the Lowe's gift cards, and unfortunately they only had a few of the larger increments left. I ended up buying eighty-three gift cards that day, mostly in $25 increments. It took me over an hour to cash out at the grocery store; each and every card had to be activated, and we hit a line limit on the cash register. It took so long that the manager took over and closed that checkout lane. I was THAT lady!

I came home with a grocery bag full of gift cards and handed them to Mark. He was confused about why, but after I explained it to him, he thanked me. He took that grocery bag full of gift cards to Lowe's and paid for our $8,000 windows. He also crashed the cash register a few times, and it took him forty-five minutes to check out. He said that he felt like we were that crazy family, but we had gotten pretty used to being that way. We were so dedicated to staying on budget that we didn't mind doing things like this. We had brand-new windows in our old home, and were $240 richer just by taking an extra hour and forty-five minutes to do things a little bit differently.

In fact, just this morning I paid for my kids' school lunches with $4 in nickels. I know the school office was probably annoyed, but I wanted to use up the coins from my kitchen coin jar. We have a saying in our house that the money jar is just like finding free money. We stick forgotten or leftover change in it daily, and use it for random expenses.

I am now okay with doing things a little bit differently in order to save a little extra money. I have come a long way from the embarrassment of using coupons and the dread of asking my cashier to take a few things off my grocery bill because I had gone over budget. My goal is being debt-free for the rest of my life, and if I have to do embarrassing things to get there, I am fine with that.

How did everything change? I was inspired. I was 100 percent on board with getting out of debt and curbing my spending addiction. Spending money wasn't important to me anymore. I decided to start spending as a reflection of my value system. I started to care where my money went. I started to plan and created a road map like I did when I was five years old. Yes, I did miss all the "stuff," but I realized that my money was better invested in what I valued.

There is a misconception that the hardest part of starting something new is just to get started. I argue that the beginning is actually the easiest part, because there is excitement and eagerness to make it work this time. In reality, the hardest part of any goal is right in the middle, when you mess up (for the millionth time) and have to figure out how to get back in the saddle.

Think about when you first set your budget. You're excited and hopeful that this is the time that it will stick and you will finally stay debt-free. Then you realize you've bounced a check, which caused an overdraft fee, and now you can't pay your credit card minimum, so you get a late fee on that. Your hard work all starts to unravel right before your eyes, and suddenly you are stuck. Pulling yourself out of that is the hardest part. Waking up that next day and starting over again is the hardest part. If you let the guilt control you, you would probably hop right off and never get started again.

If you were to see a picture of what success looks like, it would look like the letter U. You start off at the left-hand side at the top of the U and you are so excited and hopeful. As the journey goes on, you see some success, but the excitement is wearing off and you suddenly find yourself in the pit. That is the hard part, the part where you want to give up but know that if you keep on going you can achieve your goal. The key is to realize that you are in the pit and the only direction to go is up, to the other side of the U. You start to have success again, and you feel hope. Suddenly, you find yourself on the upper right-hand side of the U, and you've done it!

Success comes in steps, it isn't just a one-time thing. You don't just wake up and become a successful budgeter after being a Chronic Spender for years. It takes time and practice and messing up. It takes hard work, and dedication, and consistency. But once you come up out of that pit, you have a feeling of valor, satisfaction, and accomplishment. Don't rob yourself of that feeling by staying in the pit. Many other people get stuck in the pit, but I don't want you to be one of them.

I recently moved my two-year-old daughter out of her crib and into a toddler bed (called a "big girl bed" in our home). The strange thing is that despite being in the same room, with the same surroundings, she is suddenly terrified of her bedroom. Those boundaries of the crib railings made her feel safe and secure. When they were removed, her sense of security was altered and suddenly she was scared. Despite her continuing to ask to have her crib back, we kept her in her bed but moved it into her sisters' room. She hasn't cried since, because she has safety in knowing that her sisters will take care of her.

Since I've been budgeting for such a long time, I've gotten used to the fence around me. If I accidentally miss a budget night one month I feel scared and exposed—just like my daughter was scared when her boundaries were removed. Those securities are a part of my life now, and I don't ever want to take them for granted again.

You may be wondering what my life looks like now.

As of this writing of this book we still live in the same 1,800-square-foot house we bought when we moved out of the town house. It is tight with four kids, but in nine years we should have our mortgage paid off in full and have *zero* debt.

We have two minivans, one of them we bought with cash after negotiating with a car dealer.

Mark and I work full-time together from home on our business. We share online courses and meal plans on my website, laurengreutman.com. Once a month, I travel to New York City to go on some sort of TV show, whether it be the *Today* show, *Dr. Oz*, or *Fox News*. We pay ourselves $6,000 per month from the business as our income and still live very frugally. I still cut coupons and meal plan. I shop at thrift stores for our clothes, and every once in a while splurge on a new dress for a TV segment. Life is crazy running a business while having four small children, but I feel like I am doing exactly what God has called me to do, which is use my weaknesses to teach others. To teach you how you, too, can become a Recovering Spender.

If you want more help staying within your fence, come and join me in the Financial Renovation Community. We would love to have you a part of it!

Being a Recovering Spender doesn't mean that you will always be stressed and broke. Actually, the reverse is true. The main things you need to remember to stay in recovery are to believe in yourself, set those boundaries, and *stay inside the fence*! If you stay within your fence, you will be safe! Go outside of the fence and you may get run over by your desires, lack of self-control, and all the wants in life. Trust me, inside the fence is much safer. Within the fence your life will be so much more enjoyable.

Welcome to this side of recovery, where you can live a happy, fulfilled, and debt-free life. It is much better on this side of the fence.

Acknowledgments

This book would not have been possible without the support and encouragement of so many. I want to take some time to thank some of those people.

Thank you Mark for always being my biggest cheerleader and love of my life! For understanding my long nights at the computer, I'd like to thank my children, Andrew, Hannah, Kaylee, and Abigail. You make me a better person, and give me so much joy.

I would not be who I am today without the influence of my parents, Rick Cobello and Julie Roberts. You raised me to be independent and adventurous. I am truly thankful for all of the wisdom you have imparted on me throughout the years.

To the entire team at Hachette Book Group. Thank you for believing in me and in my vision for this book. Words cannot express my gratitude to my editor, Kate Hartson, for her professional advice and assistance in polishing this manuscript.

I am so grateful for my book agent, Scott Spiewak, from Fresh Impact Public Relations Group, and my publicist, Donna Benner, at Swoon Talent. You all helped make this dream a reality.

To all of my friends, family, and colleagues. You have sacrificed your time with me, watched my children, prayed for me, and believed in me. That means so much more to me than you will ever know!

And lastly, thank you to my readers at laurengreutman.com. Your friendship has been such an encouragement to me and my family!

Appendix A

Financial **BUCKET** List

Retirement

_____
_____
_____
_____
_____
_____
_____

Financial

_____
_____
_____
_____
_____
_____

Family

_____
_____
_____
_____
_____
_____

Housing

_____
_____
_____
_____
_____
_____

Lifestyle

_____
_____
_____
_____
_____
_____

Education

_____
_____
_____
_____
_____
_____

For more printable pages of these forms, go to
TheRecoveringSpender.com/forms

Financial **BUCKET** List

Retirement
_____
_____
_____
_____
_____
_____
_____

Financial
_____
_____
_____
_____
_____
_____

Family
_____
_____
_____
_____
_____
_____

Housing
_____
_____
_____
_____
_____

Lifestyle
_____
_____
_____
_____
_____

Education
_____
_____
_____
_____
_____

Appendix B

PERSONAL LOANS

	PERSON OWED	AMOUNT	MONTHLY PAYMENT	PAYOFF DATE
DEBT #1:		$		
DEBT #2:		$		
DEBT #3:		$		
DEBT #4:		$		
DEBT #5:		$		
DEBT #6:		$		
DEBT #7:		$		
DEBT #8:		$		
DEBT #9:		$		
DEBT #10:		$		
DEBT #11:		$		
DEBT #12:		$		
DEBT #13:		$		
DEBT #14:		$		

For more printable pages of these forms, go to
TheRecoveringSpender.com/forms

PERSONAL LOANS

	PERSON OWED	AMOUNT	MONTHLY PAYMENT	PAYOFF DATE
DEBT #1:	_____	$_____	_____	_____
DEBT #2:	_____	$_____	_____	_____
DEBT #3:	_____	$_____	_____	_____
DEBT #4:	_____	$_____	_____	_____
DEBT #5:	_____	$_____	_____	_____
DEBT #6:	_____	$_____	_____	_____
DEBT #7:	_____	$_____	_____	_____
DEBT #8:	_____	$_____	_____	_____
DEBT #9:	_____	$_____	_____	_____
DEBT #10:	_____	$_____	_____	_____
DEBT #11:	_____	$_____	_____	_____
DEBT #12:	_____	$_____	_____	_____
DEBT #13:	_____	$_____	_____	_____
DEBT #14:	_____	$_____	_____	_____

Appendix C

Month: _____

SPENDING REVIEW 1

Household

Mortgage/Rent: _____
HOA Dues: _____
Home Repairs: _____
House Cleaner: _____
_____ _____
_____ _____
_____ _____
_____ _____
_____ _____
_____ _____
_____ _____
_____ _____

Total: _____

Childcare

Day Care: _____
Babysitter: _____
Child Support: _____
_____ _____
_____ _____
_____ _____
_____ _____
_____ _____
_____ _____
_____ _____
_____ _____

Total: _____

Health Care

Health Care Premiums: _____
Doctor Visit Co-pay: _____
Medicine: _____
Supplements: _____
_____ _____
_____ _____
_____ _____
_____ _____
_____ _____

Total: _____

Food

Groceries: _____
Groceries: _____
Groceries: _____
Groceries: _____
Restaurants: _____
Restaurants: _____
Restaurants: _____
Coffee: _____
_____ _____
_____ _____
_____ _____
_____ _____
_____ _____
_____ _____

Total: _____

For more printable pages of these forms, go to
TheRecoveringSpender.com/forms

Month: _____ # SPENDING REVIEW 2

Miscellaneous

_____ _____
_____ _____
_____ _____
_____ _____
_____ _____
_____ _____
_____ _____
_____ _____
_____ _____
_____ _____
_____ _____
_____ _____
_____ _____
_____ _____
_____ _____
_____ _____
_____ _____
_____ _____
_____ _____
_____ _____
_____ _____
_____ _____
_____ _____
_____ _____
_____ _____

Total: _____

Utilities
Water Bill: _____
Electricity: _____
Natural Gas: _____
_____ _____
_____ _____

Total: _____

Cell Phone
Monthly Plan: _____
Phone Payment: _____
Total: _____

Insurance
Life Insurance: _____
Disability Insurance: _____
Other Insurance: _____
_____
_____
_____
_____
_____

Total: _____

Month: _____ # SPENDING REVIEW 3

Automotive
Gasoline: _____
Gasoline: _____
Gasoline: _____
Gasoline: _____
Car Repairs _____
Oil Change: _____

_____ _____
_____ _____
_____ _____
Total: _____

Entertainment
Date Night: _____
Movies: _____
Netflix, Hulu, etc.: _____
Mag Subscription: _____
Video Games: _____

_____ _____
_____ _____
_____ _____
Total: _____

Saving
Retirement Fund: _____
College Fund: _____
Emergency Fund: _____

Total: _____

Giving
Tithe: _____
Charity: _____

_____
Total: _____

Education
Tution: _____
Music Lessons: _____
Dance Lessons: _____
Sports: _____

_____ _____
_____ _____
Total:

Month: _____ # SPENDING REVIEW 4

Debts

_____ _____
_____ _____
_____ _____
_____ _____
_____ _____
_____ _____
_____ _____
_____ _____
_____ _____
_____ _____
_____ _____
_____ _____
_____ _____
_____ _____
_____ _____
_____ _____
_____ _____
_____ _____
_____ _____
_____ _____
_____ _____
_____ _____
_____ _____

Total: _____

Other

_____ _____
_____ _____
_____ _____
_____ _____
_____ _____
_____ _____
_____ _____
_____ _____
_____ _____
_____ _____
_____ _____
_____ _____
_____ _____
_____ _____
_____ _____
_____ _____
_____ _____
_____ _____
_____ _____
_____ _____
_____ _____
_____ _____
_____ _____

Total: _____

Month: _____ # SPENDING REVIEW 5

Summary

Household: _____
Childcare: _____
Health Care: _____
Food: _____
Miscellaneous: _____
Utilities: _____
Cell Phone: _____
Insurance: _____
Automotive: _____
Entertainment: _____
Saving: _____
Giving: _____
Education: _____
Debts: _____
Other: _____
_____
_____
_____
_____
_____
_____

Total: _____

Month: _____ # SPENDING REVIEW 1

Household

Mortgage/Rent: _____
HOA Dues: _____
Home Repairs: _____
House Cleaner: _____
_____ _____
_____ _____
_____ _____
_____ _____
_____ _____
_____ _____
_____ _____
_____ _____

Total: _____

Childcare

Day Care: _____
Babysitter: _____
Child Support: _____
_____ _____
_____ _____
_____ _____
_____ _____
_____ _____
_____ _____
_____ _____
_____ _____

Total: _____

Health Care

Health Care Premiums: _____
Doctor Visit Co-pay: _____
Medicine: _____
Supplements: _____
_____ _____
_____ _____
_____ _____
_____ _____
_____ _____

Total: _____

Food

Groceries: _____
Groceries: _____
Groceries: _____
Groceries: _____
Restaurants: _____
Restaurants: _____
Restaurants: _____
Coffee: _____
_____ _____
_____ _____
_____ _____
_____ _____
_____ _____

Total: _____

Month: _____ # SPENDING REVIEW 2

Miscellaneous

_____ _____
_____ _____
_____ _____
_____ _____
_____ _____
_____ _____
_____ _____
_____ _____
_____ _____
_____ _____
_____ _____
_____ _____
_____ _____
_____ _____
_____ _____
_____ _____
_____ _____
_____ _____
_____ _____

Total: _____

Utilities

Water Bill: _____
Electricity: _____
Natural Gas: _____

_____ _____

Total: _____

Cell Phone

Monthly Plan: _____
Phone Payment: _____
Total: _____

Insurance

Life Insurance: _____
Disability Insurance: _____
Other Insurance: _____

_____ _____
_____ _____
_____ _____
_____ _____
_____ _____
_____ _____

Total: _____

Month: _____ # SPENDING REVIEW 3

Automotive
Gasoline: _____
Gasoline: _____
Gasoline: _____
Gasoline: _____
Car Repairs _____
Oil Change: _____

_____ _____
_____ _____
_____ _____
_____ _____
Total: _____

Entertainment
Date Night: _____
Movies: _____
Netflix, Hulu, etc.: _____
Mag Subscription: _____
Video Games: _____

_____ _____
_____ _____
_____ _____
_____ _____
Total: _____

Saving
Retirement Fund: _____
College Fund: _____
Emergency Fund: _____
_____
Total: _____

Giving
Tithe: _____
Charity: _____

_____ _____
_____ _____
Total: _____

Education
Tution: _____
Music Lessons: _____
Dance Lessons: _____
Sports: _____

_____ _____
_____ _____
Total: _____

Month: _____ # SPENDING REVIEW 4

Debts

_____ _____

_____ _____

_____ _____

_____ _____

_____ _____

_____ _____

_____ _____

_____ _____

_____ _____

_____ _____

_____ _____

_____ _____

_____ _____

_____ _____

_____ _____

_____ _____

_____ _____

_____ _____

_____ _____

_____ _____

_____ _____

_____ _____

Total: _____

Other

_____ _____

_____ _____

_____ _____

_____ _____

_____ _____

_____ _____

_____ _____

_____ _____

_____ _____

_____ _____

_____ _____

_____ _____

_____ _____

_____ _____

_____ _____

_____ _____

_____ _____

_____ _____

_____ _____

_____ _____

_____ _____

_____ _____

Total: _____

Month: _____ # SPENDING REVIEW 5

Summary

Household: _____
Childcare: _____
Health Care: _____
Food: _____
Miscellaneous: _____
Utilities: _____
Cell Phone: _____
Insurance: _____
Automotive: _____
Entertainment: _____
Saving: _____
Giving: _____
Education: _____
Debts: _____
Other: _____
_____
_____
_____
_____
_____
_____
_____

Total: _____

Appendix D

BILL PRIORITIES

	EXPENSE	MONTHLY AMOUNT	INCOME REMAINING
PRIORITY #1:	_____	$_____	$_____
PRIORITY #2:	_____	$_____	$_____
PRIORITY #3:	_____	$_____	$_____
PRIORITY #4:	_____	$_____	$_____
PRIORITY #5:	_____	$_____	$_____
PRIORITY #6:	_____	$_____	$_____
PRIORITY #7:	_____	$_____	$_____
PRIORITY #8:	_____	$_____	$_____
PRIORITY #9:	_____	$_____	$_____
PRIORITY #10:	_____	$_____	$_____
PRIORITY #11:	_____	$_____	$_____
PRIORITY #12:	_____	$_____	$_____
PRIORITY #13:	_____	$_____	$_____
PRIORITY #15:	_____	$_____	$_____
PRIORITY #16:	_____	$_____	$_____
PRIORITY #17:	_____	$_____	$_____
PRIORITY #18:	_____	$_____	$_____
PRIORITY #19:	_____	$_____	$_____
PRIORITY #20:	_____	$_____	$_____
PRIORITY #21:	_____	$_____	$_____
PRIORITY #22:	_____	$_____	$_____

For more printable pages of these forms, go to
TheRecoveringSpender.com/forms

MONTHLY INCOME: _____ # BILL PRIORITIES

	EXPENSE	MONTHLY AMOUNT	INCOME REMAINING
PRIORITY #1:	_____	$_____	$_____
PRIORITY #2:	_____	$_____	$_____
PRIORITY #3:	_____	$_____	$_____
PRIORITY #4:	_____	$_____	$_____
PRIORITY #5:	_____	$_____	$_____
PRIORITY #6:	_____	$_____	$_____
PRIORITY #7:	_____	$_____	$_____
PRIORITY #8:	_____	$_____	$_____
PRIORITY #9:	_____	$_____	$_____
PRIORITY #10:	_____	$_____	$_____
PRIORITY #11:	_____	$_____	$_____
PRIORITY #12:	_____	$_____	$_____
PRIORITY #13:	_____	$_____	$_____
PRIORITY #15:	_____	$_____	$_____
PRIORITY #16:	_____	$_____	$_____
PRIORITY #17:	_____	$_____	$_____
PRIORITY #18:	_____	$_____	$_____
PRIORITY #19:	_____	$_____	$_____
PRIORITY #20:	_____	$_____	$_____
PRIORITY #21:	_____	$_____	$_____
PRIORITY #22:	_____	$_____	$_____

Notes

Resources

How to find Lauren on social media and online:

Website—www.LaurenGreutman.com
Facebook—www.facebook.com/iamthatlady
Twitter—@laurengreutman
Pinterest—www.pinterest.com/iatllauren/
Snapchat—username laurengreutman
Instagram—www.instagram.com/lauren_greutman
YouTube—www.youtube.com/iamthatlady
Podcast—*Enjoying Life on a Budget*
Website for *The Recovering Spender*—TheRecoveringSpender
.com

Links mentioned in the book:

Financial Renovation online course—www.shop.laurengreut
man.com/community
Printable forms for appendix worksheets—TheRecovering
Spender.com/Forms
Purchase Lauren's Meal plans at shop.laurengreutman.com

Books mentioned in the book:

The Life-Changing Magic of Tidying Up by Marie Kondo
A Framework for Understanding Poverty by Ruby K. Payne
Rich Dad Poor Dad by Robert Kiyosaki